REA

**DO NOT REMOVE
CARDS FROM POCKET**

Prick Up Your Ears
The Screenplay

ALAN BENNETT

adapted from
John Lahr's biography of Joe Orton

faber and faber

LONDON · BOSTON

First published in 1987 by
Faber and Faber Limited
3 Queen Square London WC1N 3AU

Typeset by Goodfellow & Egan Ltd, Cambridge
Printed in Great Britain by
Richard Clay Ltd Bungay Suffolk

British Library Cataloguing in Publication Data

Bennett, Alan, 1934–
Prick up your ears.
I. Title
822'.914   PR6052.E5
ISBN 0-571-14752-6

This is the unspoken contract of a wife and her works. In the long run wives are to be paid in a peculiar coin – consideration for their feelings. And it usually turns out this is an enormous, unthinkable inflation few men will remit, or if they will, only with a sense of being overcharged.

Elizabeth Hardwick, *Seduction and Betrayal: Women and Literature*

Introduction

The original idea for a film based on the life of Joe Orton came from John Lahr. When in 1978 he was about to publish *Prick Up Your Ears*, his biography of Orton, Lahr offered Stephen Frears and myself an option on the film rights. He anticipated that when the book was published there would be other film offers and having had an unhappy experience over an earlier book Lahr wanted to make sure Orton's story would be properly handled. Whether these other offers materialized I don't know but his caution was probably justified. One Hollywood producer who saw an early draft of the script said that he saw no problems so long as Orton was made into an American; oh, and he should of course be heterosexual.

Some writers rattle off adaptations with great facility almost as a form of relaxation. Alas I am not one of them and my initial attempts to turn the book into a film were clumsy and heavy-handed. To begin with Orton's life was unevenly documented. There was ample material covering the years from his first success as a playwright in 1964 to his death at the hands of his lover Kenneth Halliwell in 1967. Nor was it difficult to write about Orton's childhood in Leicester, since in period and background it approximated to my own in Leeds. The problem was how to tell the story of the 'lost' years, from 1951, when Orton and Halliwell first started to live together, to 1963 when Orton came to the BBC with his first completed play. It was in this period Orton was learning to write. Dramatizing the act of writing is never easy: the paper ripped from the typewriter and flung into the wastepaper basket, the overflowing ashtray and the lights burning late into the night . . . one needs no experience of the pangs of creation to be only too familiar with the screen's shorthand for it. But how else do you do it?

There was another problem. I never met Orton; he died the year before my first play was produced. I admired his plays, particularly *Entertaining Mr Sloane*, *Loot* and *The Good and Faithful Servant*, but from what I read in Lahr's biography I had mixed feelings about the man. In fact I didn't like him, or (it amounts to the same thing) I felt he wouldn't have liked me. I didn't object to the promiscuity and the cottaging; what I found hard to take was his self-assurance and the conviction (however painfully and necessarily acquired) of the superiority of his talent. Disliking Orton I took sides with Halliwell, who, having educated and sustained Orton during years of obscurity found that when his friend's talents were at last recognized he himself was left in the shadows, his contribution never publicly acknowledged. Had I met the two of them I am sure my reaction would have been different. Those who did talk of Orton's fun and charm, the perpetual bickering of Halliwell and his embarrassing bids for attention. But charm does not come off the page, nor does embarrassment, so in the first draft of the script, uncharmed by Orton and unembarrassed by Halliwell, I made the playwright the villain and the victim his friend.

This version didn't work nor was it true to the facts, so I did a second draft in which, at Lahr's suggestion, I introduced him as a character writing the biography. I also introduced myself as another character writing the screenplay of the biography, hoping in this way to come to terms with my own hostile feelings about Orton. Not surprisingly this many-layered construction didn't work either, though it was this version that in 1980 we took to a new company who were originally interested in making the film. Or making a film. Any film. I think they just fancied the idea of 'making films'. They must have done because they professed to be pleased with this baroque script, even though it was about four hours long and largely incomprehensible. More shrewdly they were banking on our selling them the rights so that they could then hack it to the shape they wanted. Fortunately at a late stage in the negotiations they let it slip that what they really had in mind was 'an English *Cage aux Folles*'. At which point we beat a hasty retreat.

There the matter rested for four years until in 1984 Zenith expressed an interest. I dusted off the script, wincing at a good deal of it and decided that what it really needed was a strong central narrator. Narrators don't normally work on film – they're a confession of some failure in the storytelling – but one that does is George Sanders as the critic Addison de Witt, who tells the story in *All About Eve*. So I wrote a third version, beginning as *All About Eve* begins at an awards ceremony with the tale being told by Orton's agent, Peggy Ramsay. It's basically that version with many additions and subtractions that is printed here.

All the various versions of the script have carried an epigraph from *Seduction and Betrayal* by Elizabeth Hardwick: 'This is the unspoken contract of a wife and her works . . .' From the start it seemed to me that the interest of Orton's and Halliwell's story was as an account of a marriage, or at any rate a first marriage. 'Ken was the first wife,' Peggy Ramsay remarks, and there is some evidence to suggest that in the final months of his life Orton was considering leaving Halliwell for someone else. The idiosyncrasies of the relationship apart, one sees many marriages like this. A young couple marry early with the husband still to make his way in the world. The wife sustains her partner through the years of struggle and endeavour, bears his first crop of children and then, just as the rewards can be expected to flow in, the husband leaves her for someone less careworn, less battle-scarred, someone more calculated to show off his new status. Never having married I find my sympathies in these circumstances going to the wife, just as, reading Lahr's book, I found they did to Halliwell. Whether that comes over as clearly in the film I'm not sure, nor am I sure that it should. To be stuck in the same room as Kenneth Halliwell for fifteen years can have been no joke.

On one point I have been unfair to Orton. In the film Orton's refusal to make public acknowledgement of his debt to Halliwell is dramatized by his refusal to take Halliwell with him to the *Evening Standard* awards. Instead he takes Peggy Ramsay. Reading Orton's diaries I find this is the reverse of the truth. Though he did take Peggy, Orton would have been happy to take his lover; it was Halliwell who refused to go. This was 1966 and had Orton and Halliwell gone together it would have been quite bold. Six years later I was at the same ceremony sitting at the same table as Edward Albee, who had brought along his friend. It was a gesture I suspect would have been taken for granted in America (and so not a gesture) but that still raised a few eyebrows here.

Orton's style is contagious and much of my first script was

ix

written in Ortonese. This would have been a mistake and in later versions I wrote it out. Orton's language is above all theatrical and not suited to a naturalistic film. (It's for this reason that the films of *Entertaining Mr Sloane* and *Loot* don't seem to me to work.) However, to write in this oblique and epigrammatic way is both a temptation and a pleasure and I have indulged myself a little, chiefly in the character of Mrs Sugden. From Orton's own diary there is almost no direct quotation, but a line like 'My vagina came up like a football' is not one for which I can take the credit.

The screenplay is not an exact transcript of the film in that I have included some scenes that had to be cut in the editing. Shorter is usually better and although we lost some good laughs there was general agreement about the cuts, with one exception. This was the final scene in which Peggy Ramsay and the Lahrs go and look at the Orton flat as it is (supposedly) today. Now a bright and cheerful place they find it lived in by a young couple. The girl is all smiles but the young man is plainly impatient with the visitors and as he ushers them out we see that in this marriage, too, there are going to be problems. This seems to me a wittier and more thoughtful ending than the scattering of the ashes which is how the film now ends. Perhaps too the young man's 'Have you seen enough?' echoes some of my own ambivalent feelings about gossip and biography, and about Orton himself.

Prick Up Your Ears opened in London in the spring of 1987. The cast was as follows:

JOE ORTON	Gary Oldman
KENNETH HALLIWELL	Alfred Molina
PEGGY RAMSAY	Vanessa Redgrave
JOHN LAHR	Wallace Shawn
ANTHEA LAHR	Lindsay Duncan
ANTHEA'S MOTHER	Joan Sanderson
MRS SUGDEN	Janet Dale
MR SUGDEN	Dave Atkins
YOUNG WOMAN	Susie Blake
YOUNG MAN	Paul Bown
ELSIE ORTON	Julie Walters
WILLIAM ORTON	James Grant
LEONIE ORTON	Frances Barber
GEORGE BARNETT	Stephen Bill
MARILYN ORTON	Sian Thomas
DOUGLAS ORTON	Karl Johnson
MADAM LAMBERT	Margaret Tyzack
EDUCATION OFFICIAL	Eric Richard
RADA CHAIRMAN	William Job
RADA JUDGES	Rosalind Knight
	Angus Mackay
RADA INSTRUCTOR	Linda Spurrier
JANET	Charlotte Wodehouse
ORTON'S RADA FRIENDS	Helena Mitchell
	Sean Pertwee
BRICKIE	Liam de Staic
PUBLISHER	Christopher Guinee
YOUTH (Kenneth)	Stevan Rimkus
MR CUNLIFFE	Charles McKeown
MISS BATTERSBY	Selina Cadell
PROSECUTING COUNSEL	Antony Carrick
POLICEMAN	Neil Dudgeon
MAGISTRATE	Bert Parnaby

PRISON PSYCHIATRIST	Richard Wilson
BBC ACTORS	Michael Mueller
	Anthony Douse
PHILIP	Noel Davis
PEGGY RAMSAY'S SECRETARY	Philippa Davies
PATRICK PROCKTOR	Derek Jarman
GALLERY OWNER	Julie Legrand
GUESTS AT PRIVATE VIEW	Jane Blackburn
	Stella Richman
	Neville Phillips
DIRECTOR (*Sloane*)	John Kane
ACTORS (*Sloane*)	Garry Cooper
	Roger Lloyd Pack
WIGMAKER	John Moffatt
YOUTH (outside lavatory)	Jonathan Phillips
MAN (outside lavatory)	Richard Ireson
BRIAN EPSTEIN	David Cardy
BEATLES' CHAUFFEUR	Mark Brignal
SIMON WARD	Steven Mackintosh
STAGE MANAGER (*Loot*)	Joanne Connelly
AWARDS CHAIRMAN	Max Stafford-Clark
MOROCCAN BOYS	Ahmed El Jheur
	Moktar Dagmouni
UNDERTAKER	David Bradley
UNDERTAKER'S BOY	Simon Adams
LABOURER	James Duggan
CHAUFFEUR	John Salthouse
POLICE INSPECTOR	Neville Smith
POLICE CONSTABLE	Spencer Leigh
MORTUARY ATTENDANT	Robin Hooper

Director	Stephen Frears
Producer	Andrew Brown
Director of Photography	Oliver Stapleton
Editor	Mick Audsley
Production Designer	Hugo Luczyc Wyhowski

INT. ORTON AND HALLIWELL'S FLAT. NIGHT. 1967
KENNETH HALLIWELL *is looking straight at the camera. He is
naked and bloody. He looks at something across the room.*
HALLIWELL: Joe?
  John?
  (*He looks back at the camera.*)

INT. ORTON AND HALLIWELL'S FLAT. DAY. 1967
*The light changes to mid-morning light and we see the door of the flat.
Sound of knocking.*
MRS SUGDEN: (*Voice over*) Hello. Mr Orton. Mr Orton?
  Mr Halliwell? Hello.
  (*Slowly a bicycle pump comes through the letterbox, pushing
  aside a fur coat on the back of the door. We see the
  CHAUFFEUR's eyes looking through the letterbox. There is a
  short pause then footsteps run rapidly downstairs. The door of the
  flat is broken down, suddenly and completely, falling flat on the
  floor, very theatrically. A POLICE INSPECTOR in raincoat
  and trilby enters, looks round.*)
INSPECTOR: Oh dear, oh dear, oh dear. Somebody here has
  been playing silly buggers.
  (*He is followed by a CONSTABLE who takes in the room and
  looks sick. He sits down, takes off his helmet and puts it on top of
  Orton's diary, which we do not particularly note, though we see
  there is a spot of blood on it.*)

INT. LANDING AND ORTON AND HALLIWELL'S FLAT.
DAY. 1967
*The POLICE PHOTOGRAPHER is just leaving. PEGGY RAMSAY
comes up the stairs, carrying her coat. She waits outside. Then turns
round and goes in backwards. The CONSTABLE is there. We see his
face as he lifts the blanket, watching PEGGY as she turns round and
looks at what is underneath the blanket. She sits down on the same
chair he had earlier sat on, with his helmet beside her. She looks, sees
the spot of blood and sees it is the diary.*

I

PEGGY: You don't look well. They have some brandy in the kitchen.
(*The* CONSTABLE *goes out of the room. She slips the diary from under the helmet, puts it under her coat and leaves.*)
CONSTABLE: (*Voice over, from kitchen*) Where?
(*He comes back into the room and she has gone. Cut to* PEGGY *passing door of Sugdens' flat. The* INSPECTOR *is on the phone.*)
INSPECTOR: One of them writes apparently.
MRS SUGDEN: (*to* MR SUGDEN) Tell him. Plays. He writes plays.
(MR SUGDEN *doesn't.* MRS SUGDEN *hands the* INSPECTOR *a fancy.*) He's had his dinner at the Savoy.
INSPECTOR: Don't know what the other one does. Hammers people's brains out, but that's in his spare time.
(PEGGY *goes on out of the house, with the diary. Fade to black.*)

INT. PEGGY RAMSAY'S OUTER OFFICE.
DAY. THE PRESENT
The door is open to the inner office. PEGGY *and* LAHR *are in the outer office. A* SECRETARY *is typing.*
PEGGY: I won't keep you a moment.

INT. PEGGY RAMSAY'S INNER OFFICE.
DAY. THE PRESENT.
PEGGY *takes the diary out of a dusty envelope, tied up with one or two exercise books. She brushes the spot of dried blood on the cover with her finger. She walks to the bookshelves, and places the diary on them.* LAHR *gets up. Approaches* PEGGY.
PEGGY: (*At the door of her office*) I can't find his diaries.
LAHR: Can't find them!
(*He goes into her office.*)
PEGGY: It is twenty years ago.
LAHR: But they'd be so valuable.
PEGGY: Yes. I don't like to think what they'd be worth.
LAHR: For a biographer!
PEGGY: Tessa's so disorganized.
(*As the door closes we catch an injured look from* TESSA.)
(LAHR *puts the tape recorder down ready to start.*)

2

PEGGY: Oh dear.

LAHR: Don't worry.

PEGGY: I can't stand those things. Every little word. One can't
possibly be natural. (*Pause.*) Is it on?
(*He nods.*)
I knew nothing about him when he first walked in. When?
My God . . . 1964! He had considerable confidence and
charm. It was his first play. Some radio thing. I thought it
was derivative. I told him so. He didn't mind.

3

INT. LAHR'S FLAT. DAY. THE PRESENT
As PEGGY *speaks we cut to* ANTHEA LAHR, *transcribing*
PEGGY's *voice from the tape recorder and typing it out.*
PEGGY: (*Voice over through cassette*) I thought it was derivative.
    I told him so. He didn't mind. Not Joe. 'I'll try and write
    you a better one, dear,' he said. I said, 'Well, that would be
    gorgeous.' As he was leaving . . .

INT. PEGGY RAMSAY'S OFFICE. DAY. THE PRESENT
PEGGY: He said 'Next time can I bring my friend?'
    And I thought 'Does he mean friend?'
    And I thought 'Yes he *does* mean friend.'
    Which was quite bold in those days.
    It was the Dark Ages. Men and men.
    And they could still put you in prison for it.
    And did, dear.

INT. PATRICK PROCKTOR'S STUDIO. DAY. 1967
ORTON *shrugs and smiles. He starts taking his clothes off. Shoes,*
trousers, shirt in that order.
ORTON: Bollock naked?
PROCKTOR: Oh no. Keep your socks on.
    (ORTON *grins. We cut to* PROCKTOR *watching him as he lies*
    on the couch, leg drawn up slightly so we do not see his cock, but
    do see his tattoo. PROCKTOR *begins to draw.*)
PEGGY: (*Voice over*) London was still quite exciting then.
    Remember that? No. No, you wouldn't.
LAHR: (*Voice over*) That was when?
PEGGY: (*Voice over*) 1967.
PROCKTOR: You're in good shape.
ORTON: It's the weights. When I die I want people to say, 'He
    was the most perfectly developed playwright of his day.'

INT. STAIRCASE UP TO PEGGY RAMSAY'S OFFICE.
DAY. 1967
ORTON *walking up some stairs. He is carrying a bag from a boutique.*
He stops outside a door marked MARGARET RAMSAY PLAY
AGENT.

4

PEGGY: (*Voice over*) Joe was having a wonderful time. His
    second play *Loot* was a smash hit.
    (ORTON *takes off his coat and pulls a fur coat out of his carrier
    bag.*)
LAHR: (*Voice over*) So he was making lots of money?
PEGGY: (*Voice over*) Oh, yes dear. Offers to do this and write that.
    (ORTON *puts on the fur coat.*)
    And he had *six months* to live.
LAHR: (*Voice over*) Wow!
    (ORTON *puts the collar of the coat up and goes into the office.*)

INT. PEGGY RAMSAY'S OFFICE. DAY. 1967
PEGGY *walks round him.*
PEGGY: Is this it? Is this my *present*?
    (ORTON *nods happily.*)
    It's *terrible*, darling.
ORTON: It was fourteen quid.
PEGGY: Joe! I said splash out.
ORTON: Cheap clothes suit me, they always have. It's because
    I'm from the gutter.
    (ORTON *stares at himself happily in the mirror.*)
PEGGY: A contract from New Zealand.
ORTON: (*Incredulous*) *New Zealand*?
PEGGY: I know, dear, but we're not going to think about it. Now
    am I right in thinking we're still interested in writing the
    Beatles script?
ORTON: Oh, yes . . .
PEGGY: Then why don't I call Brian now and set up a meeting?
    (ORTON *looks delighted.*)
ORTON: Smashing!
    (*She stops dialling.*)
PEGGY: Now, is it *Epsteen* or *Epstine*? Better wait.
    (*She hesitates and then puts the phone down.*)
    Americans are so sensitive about their names.
ORTON: He's not American, is he?
PEGGY: (*Who hadn't known*) Well, he moves in that world. We
    shall see each other later.
    (ORTON *makes a small face.*)

5

ORTON: I hope people come.
PEGGY: They will. I've put out a three-line whip.
ORTON: (*Gratefully*) Peggy.
PEGGY: How is he?
ORTON: Fine. He's fine.

EXT. NOEL ROAD. DUSK. 1967
ORTON *walks down the street.*

INT. STAIRS TO ORTON AND HALLIWELL'S FLAT,

25 NOEL ROAD. DUSK. 1967
ORTON *goes up slowly.*

INT. ORTON AND HALLIWELL'S FLAT. DUSK. 1967
The walls of the flat are covered in a collage made up of
illustrations from art books, colour magazines, etc. The effect is
claustrophobic. ORTON *enters.* HALLIWELL, *without his wig, is*
oppressively silent. ORTON, *still in his coat, opens his letters which*
are on his glossy, white desk. ORTON *is seemingly oblivious of the*
silence.
ORTON: (*Showing him the coat*) Well?
HALLIWELL: It is five o'clock. It's a quarter *past* five.
ORTON: Only fourteen pounds. Peggy hates it.
HALLIWELL: That's where you've been.
ORTON: She likes you. Peggy is one of your few fans.
  (ORTON *gets a pan from the stove, sniffs the contents, then starts*
  eating them with a spoon while looking at the letters on his desk.)
ORTON: Any calls?
HALLIWELL: (*Hands him a note of the calls.*) I was worried stiff.
ORTON: Why? It doesn't start till nine.
HALLIWELL: The point about irrational behaviour is that it is
  irrational. I don't worry about anything. I just worry.
  (HALLIWELL *sits on the bed, head against the wall.* ORTON
  sits down beside him, similarly. ORTON *puts one leg over*
  HALLIWELL'*s.*)
  Stop that.
ORTON: You stop being such a bilious queen.
HALLIWELL: I ought to be there by eight to check all the
  arrangements. I'm frightened nobody's going to come.
ORTON: They'll come.
  (*Pause.*)
HALLIWELL: 'What sort of day have you had, Kenneth?'
ORTON: What sort of day have you had, Kenneth?
HALLIWELL: Well, not unproductive, Joe, actually. I caught up
  on a big backlog of dusting. Then I slipped out to the end of
  the road to replenish our stock of cornflakes. When I got
  back I rinsed a selection of your soiled underclothes by
  which time it was four o'clock, the hour of your scheduled

7

return. When you failed to appear I redeemed the shining
hour by cutting my toenails. What do you expect me to
fucking do, shag the Dimplex?

ORTON: You can still be quite funny.

HALLIWELL: 'Still'.

(ORTON *opens a drawer of his desk to put in a letter and sees his
diary there. There is a slight suggestion in his face that it is not
where he remembers leaving it.*)

ORTON: You've been reading my diary?

HALLIWELL: No.

ORTON: Why not? I would.

(HALLIWELL *goes to a cupboard and, from a string behind the door, takes an Old Etonian tie and puts it on.* ORTON *changes into a clean T-shirt.* HALLIWELL, *behind him, puts on his wig.*)

(*Over this action* PEGGY'S *interview with* LAHR *continues.*)

PEGGY: (*Voice over*) They lived in Islington.

LAHR: (*Voice over*) Isn't that very fashionable?

PEGGY: (*Voice over*) Not then, dear.

LAHR: (*Voice over*) In an apartment?

PEGGY: (*Voice over*) Hardly. It was a cupboard!

HALLIWELL: All right?

ORTON: (*Seeing him in the mirror*) Smashin'.

(*But looking critically at himself he takes off his jeans, removes his underpants and then puts his jeans back on again, as* HALLIWELL *puts on some make-up.* HALLIWELL *retrieves the underpants and puts them to wash as* ORTON *puts on a leather jacket.* ORTON *now puts on a jaunty little cap.*)

Can we go past the theatre?

HALLIWELL: Oh *no*. I knew you'd say that. I knew. This was supposed to be my night.

ORTON: (*As the door closes*) Actually, I just want to get out of this fucking room.

(*As they go downstairs we see the room in its entirety.*)

HALLIWELL: (*Voice over*) I'd better have my valium now.

ORTON: (*Voice over*) Give us a couple.

INT/EXT. NOEL ROAD. DUSK. 1967

MRS SUGDEN, *the middle-aged occupant of the bottom flat, is at her door.* MR SUGDEN *comes up behind her. She addresses* HALLIWELL *and* ORTON *as they come down the stairs.*

MRS SUGDEN: Name in the paper again last night. Mr Sugden says you're halfway to being a household word. Kenneth looks smart. Don't look at me. I'm not washed.

(*She looks through the door as they go out.*)

Going out to supper. Candlelit probably. It's one function after another.

(MR SUGDEN *comes to the door and watches.*)

They've got the world at their feet.

EXT. CRITERION THEATRE. NIGHT. 1967
ORTON *and* HALLIWELL *pass by the theatre. We see the neon sign which reads:*

'OUTRAGEOUSLY FUNNY'
LOOT
BY JOE ORTON

There is a HOUSE FULL *sign outside the Box Office.*

INT. KING'S ROAD GALLERY. NIGHT. 1967
A small and not very smart gallery, possibly subterranean and a bit damp. Halliwell's collages are ranged round the walls. A screen made by Halliwell is also on show. A table of glasses filled with white wine, cocktail snacks. The GALLERY OWNER *is an eager woman, determinedly cheerful.* ORTON *and* HALLIWELL *stand in the middle of the gallery, which is otherwise empty.*

GALLERY OWNER: (*Looks at watch.*) Early yet.
    (*She goes and looks at one of the collages with* HALLIWELL.)
    When I was hanging them I kept thinking Schwitters.
    Wrong?
HALLIWELL: Not entirely. Because when I first started . . .
    (*Cut to* PEGGY *and* PHILIP *coming into the gallery entrance and down the stairs.*)
PHILIP: It would be in a cellar.
PEGGY: Shut up. This is our 'Let's be nice to Ken' evening.
GALLERY OWNER: Ah! The avalanche begins.
    (*The* GALLERY OWNER *breaks away and goes to the table to get glasses for* PEGGY *and* PHILIP.)
PEGGY: We came together.
ORTON: Always the best way. Philip.
    (*He kisses* PHILIP.)
PHILIP: Joe.
PEGGY: Ken.
    (*She kisses* HALLIWELL.)
PHILIP: Kenneth. Your big day. How are you, Joe?
PEGGY: Now, where are these pictures?
    (*She takes* HALLIWELL's *arm and he walks round with her, leaving* ORTON *with* PHILIP, *who stands in the middle of the*

room, surveying the pictures but not very interested. More people are arriving.)

ORTON: (*Muttering to* PHILIP) Nice of you to come.

PHILIP: Girls must stick together. I had a friend once who was in soft furnishings. The times I've trailed round the Ideal Home Exhibition!

ORTON: I've had an invitation from the Lord Mayor of London. It's a banquet for those eminent in the Arts and Sciences.

PHILIP: How exciting.

ORTON: It's just because I've sold the film rights to *Loot*. I'm as rich as they are so they invite me to their rubbishy dinner.

PHILIP: I believe they have excellent turtle soup. (*Pause.*) Who's paying for this?

(ORTON *says nothing but it's plain that he is.*)

You're a saint.

(*The* GALLERY OWNER *passes.*)

GALLERY OWNER: Success! Our first sale.

HALLIWELL: Peggy's bought my cat screen. And I've almost sold another.

(*He goes to someone looking at the picture as* PEGGY *joins* ORTON *and* PHILIP.)

ORTON: You've no need to.

PEGGY: I *like* it.

PHILIP: You've no need to either. Not any more. You don't owe him anything, Joe. Leave him.

ORTON: I can't. No, I couldn't.

(PEGGY *goes to the table and signs a cheque and we see the* GALLERY OWNER *put a red dot on the screen as* PEGGY'S *interview with* LAHR *continues.*)

LAHR: (*Voice over*) And was he going to leave him?

PEGGY: (*Voice over*) No shortage of offers. (*She sighs.*) I don't know.

LAHR: (*Voice over*) Could he have left him?

PEGGY: (*Voice over*) You're married. How can you tell?

WOMAN: He was in prison you know. They both were.

MAN: What for? Sex?

WOMAN: (*Shrugs.*) I suppose that's where he learned it. Therapy.

(*There is a group around* ORTON *chatting and laughing with fewer and fewer people looking at the collages.*)
And what do you do?

HALLIWELL: I'm the artist.

WOMAN: Really? They're . . . very unusual.

GALLERY OWNER: It seems to be going well.

HALLIWELL: Have we sold any more?

GALLERY OWNER: No, but I'm getting lots of enthusiasm.

WOMAN 2: Isn't that Joe Orton?

HALLIWELL: Yes.

WOMAN 2: I loved *Loot*.

HALLIWELL: The title was mine actually. I give him all his titles. I'm his personal assistant.

WOMAN 2: Really? I don't care for these at all. (*Refers to the collages.*) What does that entail?

HALLIWELL: It entails washing his underwear. It entails taking his jumpers to Sketchley's. It entails poaching his fucking eggs and it entails reading his manuscripts and finding every single thing I have ever thought or said has been included.

WOMAN 2: (*Who has not been listening*) That must be very rewarding.

HALLIWELL: (*Shouting*) If you are referring, madam, to the occasional bout of mutual masturbation, no, it is not rewarding at all.

PEGGY: (*Rescuing* HALLIWELL) I love my screen.

HALLIWELL: Honestly?

PEGGY: (*Putting her arm through his*) Ken.
(*The gallery empties as we jump forward in time with* PEGGY.)
(*Voice over*) People tried, you see. But Ken was so touchy. Nobody could understand it. One of them so bright and funny and clever, the other such a plain, envious failure . . . Oh, that's not fair . . . It's just that people shouldn't marry young, that's all.

INT. UNDERGROUND STATION. NIGHT. 1967
ORTON *and* HALLIWELL *are going down in a crowded lift.*
A good-looking YOUTH *has caught* ORTON'S *eye.*

HALLIWELL: 'How do you justify your existence?' 'I'm Joe Orton's friend.' As if it's a profession. It's not a profession. It's a fucking full-time job, but it's not a profession.
(*The lift stops and as the passengers go down the tunnel to the platform* ORTON *hangs back.* HALLIWELL *goes on. The* YOUTH *stops, looks back at* ORTON *then turns and follows him.* HALLIWELL *stops and watches the successful pick-up then goes on alone.*)

INT. EMPTY UNDERGROUND STATION. NIGHT. 1967
Close-up on ORTON's *face, waiting. The* YOUTH *appears.*
We hold on YOUTH's *face and see* ORTON's *hand go out of frame*
and hear a zip go down. A faint smile spreads over the YOUTH's *face.*

LAHR: (*Voice over*) Was this customary?

PEGGY: (*Voice over*) Oh yes! According to the diaries practically a
   daily occurrence.

LAHR? (*Voice over*) But you lost his diaries.

PEGGY: (*Voice over*) Oh yes.

INT. ORTON AND HALLIWELL'S FLAT. NIGHT. 1967
HALLIWELL *sits in the flat waiting for* ORTON's *return. He*
telephones.

INT. PEGGY RAMSAY'S OFFICE. NIGHT. 1967
Close-up on PEGGY.
PEGGY: I just called in to get some contracts. No. I haven't seen
   him. I thought he left with you. Of course I wanted it. I
   wouldn't have bought it if I hadn't. I shall have it here in the
   office. Yes, if he rings I'll tell him. Bye.
   (*She puts the phone down looking a little shamefaced. Camera*
   pulls out and we see ORTON *is there with* PHILIP. ORTON
   seems oblivious of the call, or deliberately so.)
PHILIP: Then what?
ORTON: Then he did the same for me.
   (PHILIP *looks interested.* PEGGY *less so.*)
PEGGY: Can we eat? I'm starving.
ORTON: I write it all down. All the sex. It's all in my diaries.
PEGGY: How did he know you were here?
ORTON (*Shrugs.*) You do, don't you? When you're in that state.
   You know everything.
PHILIP: I don't know how you stand it.

INT. LAHRS' FLAT. EVENING. THE PRESENT
ANTHEA *is preparing supper. She is alone in the flat.* LAHR *comes*
in, late.
LAHR: Sorry.
   (ANTHEA *says nothing.*)
   I've got the melon.
   (*She takes it from him and cuts it in two, scooping out the seeds.*)
   Any calls?
   (*She wordlessly hands him the paper.*)
   I'm sorry.
   (*The doorbell rings.*)
ANTHEA: Shit.
   (*She whips her pinny off. He puts his coat back on and opens the*
   door. PEGGY *is on the doorstep with a parcel containing the*
   diaries.)

15

LAHR: You found us.

PEGGY: Eventually.

LAHR: I just got in myself.

(LAHR *brings* PEGGY *in.*)

This is my wife, Anthea. Miss Ramsay.

PEGGY: I think it's perhaps Peggy.

ANTHEA: Why don't you get Miss Ramsay a drink, John? White wine?

PEGGY: White wine. You're not American?

ANTHEA: No. He's American. John's American. He is. I'm not.

PEGGY: Yes. I think I've just about got that straight.

(LAHR *and* PEGGY *retire to sofa while* ANTHEA *finishes off preparing the meal. We see from* ANTHEA'*s point of view* PEGGY *unwrapping her parcel and taking out the exercise books, etc., which form* ORTON'*s diaries.* ANTHEA *mashes potatoes, strains sprouts, etc.*)

PEGGY: Now these are the diaries. You must guard them with your life.

ANTHEA: We can eat.

(*They come to the table.* ANTHEA *is lighting the candles. They are eating melon.*)

PEGGY: (*Turns to Lahr.*) Urinals figure largely, of course.

ANTHEA: Sugar?

(PEGGY *puts some on.*)

PEGGY: The more insalubrious the circumstances, the more Joe seemed to enjoy it.

ANTHEA: Ginger?

PEGGY: His first taste of sex, or the first that he records, seems to have taken place in a cinema lavatory in Leicester at the age of fourteen. The film was *My Favourite Brunette*.

LAHR: Bob Hope and Dorothy Lamour.

PEGGY: Quite. Joe says he came all down the man's raincoat. Lovely melon.

LAHR: Oh, thank you.

(ANTHEA *clears the plates.*)

I'll set Anthea to work transcribing these then you can have the originals back. What is this?

PEGGY: This is the film script he was writing for the Beatles that final summer.

INT. ORTON AND HALLIWELL'S FLAT. DAY. 1967
ORTON *answering the phone in shirt and pants.*

INT. PEGGY RAMSAY'S OFFICE. DAY. 1967
PEGGY: Darling I'm about to get Brian Epstein on the phone. When can we set up a meeting?
SECRETARY: (*Calling*) Not there, Miss Ramsay. On the coast.
PEGGY: (*Picking up the phone*) When you say he's on the coast, dear, do you mean he's in Brighton?
(*We only hear* PEGGY's *end of the conversation.*)
Well, when he gets back and has shaken the sand out of his shoes, perhaps you could ask him to call me.
(*She puts the phone down.*) Slut.

INT. ORTON AND HALLIWELL'S FLAT. DAY. 1967
We only hear ORTON's *end of the call.*
ORTON: (*To* PEGGY) I've started on the script for the Beatles. I'm using some of a novel I wrote years ago. I'm surprised how good it is. (*He puts down the phone and goes to put his trousers on.*)
HALLIWELL: You didn't write this. *We* wrote it.
ORTON: So what were you planning on doing? Selling it to Warner Brothers?
(ORTON *goes back to work, but can't as* HALLIWELL *is now pacing the room.*)
HALLIWELL: I wouldn't care if you gave me some credit. If you only said . . . told people I helped you. Tell the Beatles I helped you.
ORTON: You're not being much help now. Have you nothing to do?
HALLIWELL: (*Who is cleaning up*) Look at me.
ORTON: I hate your pinafore number.
HALLIWELL: So you do it. Try a spot of post-coital dusting

17

yourself. (*Shoving the mop or whatever at him, shouting.*)
It always has to be me!
(*A knock at the door. Sudden silence.*)
(*Whispering*) Who's this?
(ORTON *gives a 'search me' shrug.*)
It's the police. It's one of your pick-ups. Your sex life has
caught up with you. Now you're going to have to pay.
(ORTON *gets up wearily and opens the door. It is*
MRS SUGDEN.)

MRS SUGDEN: I thought you might like a preview of my frock.
It's for the firm's get-together in a month or two's time. The

venue's not definite yet, but it's thought to be one of the
leading London hotels.
(*She parades in a gaudy full-length dress of some printed
material.*)
There's been some dispute about the design. It's a floral
motif, obviously. All hand done. Only I say these are roses.
And Mr Sugden will insist they're peonies.

HALLIWELL: This could be a lily.

ORTON: Looks more like a rhododendron to me.

MRS SUGDEN: That's a thought. I'll go and try that one out on
Clifford. Do you notice I'm limping? Spilt a hot drink over

my dress. My vagina came up like a football.
(*She goes.* ORTON *and* HALLIWELL *are hysterical with laughter and collapse on the bed.*)

ORTON: If you were successful . . . so successful you couldn't walk down the street, what would you do? I'm thinking of the Beatles.

HALLIWELL: I'd have a home in the country. Servants.

ORTON: I wouldn't. I'd just screw everything in sight.
(HALLIWELL *touches* ORTON.)
Lay off. Have a wank.

HALLIWELL: (*Furiously tidying up the flat*) Have a wank? Have a wank? I can't just have a wank. I need three days' notice to have a wank. You can just stand there and do it. Me, it's like organizing D-Day. Forces have to be assembled, magazines bought, the past dredged for some suitably unsavoury episode the dog-eared thought of which can still produce a faint flicker of desire. 'Have a wank.' It'd be easier to raise the *Titanic*.
(ORTON *typing.*)

HALLIWELL: And don't write it down.

ORTON: It's only my diary. Do you read it?

HALLIWELL: I've told you. No.

ORTON: My mum did. I used to have to put the dirty bits in shorthand. Only time it's been of any use.

INT. PEGGY RAMSAY'S OFFICE. DAY. THE PRESENT
PEGGY *is on the phone.*
PEGGY: I'm sorry, I can't help you. My secretary does shorthand, but I'm on my own here.
(*Her* SECRETARY *puts some papers on her desk.*)
You'll just have to use your imagination.

INT. LAHRS' FLAT. DAY. THE PRESENT
ANTHEA *puts the phone down. Her* MOTHER *is in the flat.*
ANTHEA: Mother, didn't you once do shorthand?
MOTHER: Yes, for about five minutes.
ANTHEA: It's this playwright John is writing about. He went to secretarial school as a boy and took shorthand. This is his diary.

20

(ANTHEA *shows it to her* MOTHER.)
He keeps going into shorthand, you see.
MOTHER: Yes. It was a long time ago, dear. I never got the diploma.
(*She studies the text.*)
ANTHEA: 'Woke up late. Did not go to school. Told Mum I felt sick. When she had gone to work I listened to Housewives' Choice.'
MOTHER: '. . . then went into Mum's bedroom and arranged her dressing-table mirrors and . . . had a lovely long slow . . . wink.
ANTHEA: Wink? Are you sure that's an 'i'?
MOTHER: No, dear. I'm not sure at all. . . . 'Read all morning, but got another hard-on. Just putting soap on it when Mum came in. Said I thought I had a spot coming. Mum quiet all through meal.' I should think so. Do they go on like this?
ANTHEA: No. The early ones stop just when his life got interesting.
MOTHER: Sounds quite interesting already. Where's John?
ANTHEA: Gone to Leicester to see the sister . . .

EXT. FAYHURST ROAD, LEICESTER. DAY. THE PRESENT
LAHR *walks towards a house on a poor council estate.*
ANTHEA: (*Voice over*) . . . to look at the house where Joe was brought up.
(*An* ASIAN WOMAN *comes out.*)
LAHR: Hello. Was this the Orton house?
(*She doesn't understand. An* OLD WOMAN *next door watches.*
LAHR *walks away.*)
OLD WOMAN: Ask me, young man. I'm English. Ask me.

INT. LEONIE ORTON'S SITTING ROOM. DAY. THE PRESENT
Comfortable sitting room. Some books. Pictures of ORTON.
LEONIE: I hated that house. There was no love in it. No wonder he couldn't wait to get out. In those days if you wanted to be an actor and you were from Leicester you had to get rid of your accent. Not that Mum knew about the acting. She just wanted John to talk posh.

LAHR: You still call him 'John'?

LEONIE: (*Out of vision*) That was his name when we were little. It was after he was famous he was Joe.

EXT. MADAM LAMBERT'S HOUSE. DAY. 1950
ORTON, *aged 16, knocks at a little semi-detached house with a brass plate on the gate. An impressive matronly* WOMAN *opens the door.*

ORTON: Mrs Lambert?

MADAM LAMBERT: *Madam* Lambert.

INT. MADAM LAMBERT'S HOUSE. DAY. 1950
They have come inside. She is looking at his letter.

MADAM LAMBERT: You are anxious to improve your diction?

ORTON: (*Mutters*) Yes, Madam Lambert.

MADAM LAMBERT: What is your chosen field?

ORTON: I want to be an actor.

MADAM LAMBERT: Indeed? Leicester has produced some fine actors. Leicester is the home town of Richard Attenborough. Tea? You'll find a biscuit in the barrel.

INT. MADAM LAMBERT'S HOUSE. DAY. 1950
ORTON *sits with a book open. He has just been reading.*

MADAM LAMBERT: . . . movement, elocution. These I can teach you. The arts proper to the stage: how to smoke a cigarette with poise, elegance and, above all, conviction. The powder compact as a means of expression. Go to any production in the West End and you will see these arts brought to a pitch of perfection. But all that is as nothing without the one essential requirement.

ORTON: I have the money.

MADAM LAMBERT: Money! Pish. I am not speaking of money. I am speaking of talent. Judging by what you've read, you have no talent. No talent whatsoever.

ORTON: I still want to learn.

MADAM LAMBERT: Bravo! No marks for talent. Full marks for the Dunkirk Spirit.
(*She toasts him with the teacup.*)

INT. ORTON'S BEDROOM. DAY. 1950
ORTON *is pinning up a poster of an amateur performance on the wall.*

INT. ORTON HOUSE: LIVING ROOM. DAY. 1950
ELSIE ORTON *is raging.*
ELSIE: Bloody plays!
   (*She looks down at a stained bedspread.*)

INT. LEONIE'S HOUSE. DAY. 1980
LEONIE: My Mum didn't have much of a horizon. She'd have
   liked him a civil servant. A suit every day of his life.

INT. ORTON HOUSE: LIVING ROOM. DAY. 1950
ELSIE: Next time tell them to provide you with a costume.
   Using our bedspread. It's wicked.

INT. ORTON'S BEDROOM. DAY. 1950
ORTON *looks at his scrapbook. He has obviously been in several plays
by now as there are various pictures and notices.*
ELSIE: (*Voice over*) You'll clean it! Covering it with distemper.
   It's ruined. Bloody ruined.
   (*She comes to the foot of the stairs.*)
   (*Voice over*) I bet Dirk Bogarde didn't distemper his mother's
   bedspread!
   (*He closes his scrapbook.*)
   (*Voice over*) Bloody disgusting. And get some clothes on.
   Walking around like Sabu. I don't know where to look.
   (*There is a knocking at the front door and a sudden silence.*)

INT. ORTON HOUSE: HALL. DAY. 1950
ELSIE, *at the foot of the stairs. Point of view from top of the flight.*
ELSIE: (*Whispering*) John. John.
   (ORTON *goes to the top of the stairs.*)
ORTON: What?
ELSIE: Somebody at the door. Fetch me my teeth.
   (ORTON *goes to the bathroom and gets her tooth glass and takes
   it downstairs. She jiggles the glass and puts them in.*)
   It'll be the gas man. I never paid.

23

(*She retreats into the room as the banging on the door gets louder. Suddenly the door opens.*)

OFFICIAL: Good afternoon. I am a council official. I have come about your lad.

ELSIE: Why? What's he done? (*Turning to* ORTON) What have you done?

OFFICIAL: Some Shakespeare, that's what he's done. Taken a very good part. He has favourably impressed a prominent member of the Education Committee.

ELSIE: Yes. In our bedspread.

(ELSIE *is dumbfounded. The door opens and* WILLIAM ORTON *comes in.* LEONIE *ventures out from under the table.*)

WILLIAM: Who's this?

OFFICIAL: Good afternoon.

ELSIE: This is my husband. Ignore him.

OFFICIAL: Your son is a born actor.

ELSIE: An actor? But he went to Clarks College. He has done shorthand. He has a badge on his blazer.

OFFICIAL: This boy will never make a typist.

WILLIAM: He can do forty words a minute.

ELSIE: Shut up.

OFFICIAL: He must take up a dramatic career.

ELSIE: But I've sacrificed all down the line in order for him to land a job in an office.

(*She is gathering up the spoilt bedspread as she is saying this.*)

OFFICIAL: Mrs Orton, your lad must go in for a scholarship to RADA.

WILLIAM: RADA?

OFFICIAL: The Royal Academy of Dramatic Art.

INT. MADAM LAMBERT'S HOUSE. LIVING ROOM.
DAY. 1950

MADAM LAMBERT: (*Putting down* The Lady) RADA?

EXT. ORTON HOUSE. BY GARDEN FENCE. DAY. 1950

ELSIE: (*To* NEIGHBOUR) RADA! The Royal Academy of Dramatic Art.

INT. ELSIE'S BEDROOM. DAY. 1950
ORTON *is in front of his mother's three-way bedroom mirror, so that he is pictured three times.*
ORTON: RADA!

INT. RADA BUILDING. AFTERNOON. 1950
Auditorium at RADA. ORTON *is acting Smee and Captain Hook from* Peter Pan, *playing both parts. The* JUDGES *sit at a table halfway up the auditorium. They laugh occasionally.*
ORTON: (*Hook:*) Do you know who I'm looking for, Smee? (*Smee:*)Tell me again, Captain. (*Hook:*) I'm looking for a boy, Smee. (*Smee:*) What kind of boy, Captain? (*Hook:*) A wicked boy, a heartless boy, a boy who never ate his rice pudding. (*Smee:*) Oh horror. Can there be such boys? (*Hook:*) Aye, there can. It was a boy like that cut off my arm and gave it to the crocodiles. His name was Peter Pan. (*Another voice:*) Tick-tock, tick-tock, tick-tock.
CHAIRMAN: (*A voice out of the gloom*) You've had some amateur experience, I gather. Tell us about it.
(*They confer, while* ORTON *shades his eyes and tries to see them.*)
ORTON: I . . . started off in *Richard III.*
VOICE: (*Voice over*) As what?
ORTON: A messenger.
(*Laughter.*)
CHAIRMAN: Well, that was most original, Mr Orton. You've done very well.
(ORTON *leaves.*)

INT. RADA BUILDING. DAY. 1950
RADA auditorium. HALLIWELL *emerges from the darkness and stands in a pool of light on the stage. His camel-hair coat is draped over his shoulders. There is a pause before he embarks on a speech from* Hamlet. *A suppressed groan from the panel.*
MAN: Rather old.
WOMAN: (*Rustle of a form.*) Not as old as he looks.
ANOTHER MAN: Useful to have someone as old as that, just for casting.

WOMAN: We seem to be taking practically anything that stands up.
> (*Camera closes in on* HALLIWELL.)
MAN: At least he's got the coat.

INT. RADA REHEARSAL ROOM. DAY. 1951
The STUDENTS *are doing improvisations of the movements of various animals, hens, penguins, etc. A* WOMAN INSTRUCTOR *is moving round the class and comes on* TWO STUDENTS *rubbing up against one another.*
INSTRUCTOR: And what are you?
STUDENTS: Cats, miss.
> (*She claps her hands.*)
INSTRUCTOR: We're going to change the exercise slightly. I've
> got a cat here.
> (*She mimes stroking a cat.*)
> Here you are. Catch it.
> (*She mimes throwing it to a* STUDENT, *who catches it, strokes it and passes it on. It reaches* HALLIWELL, *who makes a great fuss of it, then begins to get angry when it scratches him and eventually strangles it in an awesome display of fury which silences the class, all, that is, except* ORTON, *who laughs loudly.*)

INT. RADA BUILDING: ENTRANCE. DAY. 1951
The entrance hall is empty except for HALLIWELL *who is looking fixedly at the notice board, examining the timetable.* ORTON *comes in, looks at the clock and sits down to wait for his friend. Silence.*
HALLIWELL: Movement. Enunciation. Breath Control.
> (*Pauses.*) It's all so wildly dated. Don't you agree?
ORTON: (*Startled at being spoken to*) Er . . . yes . . . yes . . .
HALLIWELL: Still, I suppose the beginners find it useful.
> (*He turns around at last and favours* ORTON *with a look of superior benevolence.*)
ORTON: Are you new to London?
HALLIWELL: Hardly. A small legacy has enabled me to spend
> several weekends at the Strand Palace.
ORTON: Hotels are a closed book to me.
HALLIWELL: You'll like the Strand Palace. We might venture
> there for coffee one evening.

(ORTON's *companions come down the stairs. Another* BOY *and his* GIRL, *and* JANET, ORTON's *girl.*)

JANET: Ready?

(*They are going out when* ORTON *turns back.*)

ORTON: We're off over the South Bank. The Festival.

(JANET *is dismayed.* HALLIWELL *considers.*)

HALLIWELL: It might be amusing, I suppose.

ORTON: (*Trying to be sophisticated*) Yes. The plebs at their simple pleasures.

(HALLIWELL *precedes them through the door as* JANET *mouths to* ORTON.)

JANET: What did you ask him for?

ORTON: He's got a . . . (*Makes steering wheel motions.*)

EXT. STREET. DUSK. 1951

HALLIWELL's *open car riding along beneath the Festival lights.* HALLIWELL *is driving.* ORTON *is sitting in the front seat with* JANET *on his knee. The other* TWO STUDENTS *are perched behind.*

EXT. FESTIVAL OF BRITAIN. NIGHT. 1951

ORTON, HALLIWELL, JANET *and* TWO STUDENTS *are walking through a park. Fairy lights in the trees, loudspeakers attached to trees. Music playing (or they are moving towards distant music and the lights of an open-air dance floor).* PEOPLE *are lying on the grass in sleeping bags; rows of people. Some locked in each other's arms.* HALLIWELL *strides ahead.*

HALLIWELL: (*Declaiming*) 'Let us go then, you and I
When the evening is spread out against the sky
Like a patient etherized upon a table . . .'

(ORTON *is looking at the lovers and sleepers.*)

JANET: Come on.

(ORTON *comes running up beside* HALLIWELL.)

ORTON: You know, some of these people are . . well . . . having sexual intercourse.

HALLIWELL: Fucking you mean? Well, what do you expect? Many of them are from Australia.

(*A* SAILOR *passes by.* HALLIWELL *looks at him.* ORTON *sees and looks at* HALLIWELL. *They walk on and come to an*

27

outdoor dance floor with couples dancing.)

LAHR: (*Voice over*) What was the Festival of Britain?

PEGGY: (*Voice over*) Oh, that was when it all came off the ration.

LAHR: (*Voice over*) You mean food and stuff.

PEGGY: (*Voice over*) Life, dear. Sex. Everything. Only they didn't, of course.

EXT. FESTIVAL OF BRITAIN. BALCONY
(OR HUNGERFORD BRIDGE). NIGHT. 1951
ORTON *and* JANET *go to the wall by the river and kiss*.
JANET: I wish he'd never come. I wanted it to be just us.

(ORTON *kisses her again, interested in the sex but not the conversation.*)
John.
(ORTON *is trying to touch her up. During the scene the lights of the Festival gradually go off, section by section.*)
No.

ORTON: Why?

JANET: Not here. People are looking.

ORTON: Fuck people.

JANET: You can't live like that, John. I want to take things gradually.

ORTON: I don't.

JANET: You don't know what life's like, you.

ORTON: And I'm not going to find out at this rate either.
(*He leaves* JANET *and goes back to* HALLIWELL, *who is now looking at the Festival where the only thing left glowing between them in the darkness is the Skylon. Suddenly the Skylon goes out. There is a moment of total darkness, then the fireworks explode in the sky, illuminating the upturned faces of* ORTON *and* HALLIWELL.)

INT. CAR. LONDON STREET. DAY. 1953
ORTON *and* HALLIWELL *come out of gents' outfitters and get into the car.* ORTON *is wearing new clothes.*

ORTON: Thank you.

HALLIWELL: Cheap clothes suit you. It's because you're from the gutter.
(ORTON *and* HALLIWELL *drive along in Halliwell's car with the hood down.*)
It occurs to me. Since we've so little in common, why don't we share a flat?

ORTON: I've said I'll move in with Janet.

INT. ORTON AND HALLIWELL'S FLAT: STAIRCASE.
DAY. 1953
MRS SUGDEN *taking* HALLIWELL *and* ORTON *up the staircase.*

MRS SUGDEN: This is the room.

29

INT. ORTON AND HALLIWELL'S FLAT: BEDROOM.
DAY. 1953
HALLIWELL *walks around.* ORTON *stays outside the door with*
MRS SUGDEN.

ORTON: I'm only looking. I'm fixed up elsewhere.

HALLIWELL: Is it a northern light?

MRS SUGDEN: Never had any complaints. It's in dire need of
decorating of course.

HALLIWELL: What's that smell?

MRS SUGDEN: Air freshener. The carpet came from Reading
originally. Friends, are you?

ORTON: Students.

MRS SUGDEN: I've nothing against friendship. It's the most
wonderful thing in the world. Within reason.

ORTON: I'm only looking.

(HALLIWELL *is testing the beds.*)

HALLIWELL: They say Islington's coming up.

MRS SUGDEN: It is. They've turned the greengrocer's into an
antique shop, and the pub does salad.

HALLIWELL: What do you think?

ORTON: I think I ought to keep an open mind.

MRS SUGDEN: Nice woolly.

(*She strokes* ORTON's *new jumper.*)
A glance at the toilet might clinch it.
(*She shows* HALLIWELL *the toilet while* ORTON *remains
looking at the room, obviously liking it.*)
(*Voice over*) Every Wednesday I give the whole place a good
going over with Dettol. You ought to feel secure in your
mind in a toilet.
(MRS SUGDEN *and* HALLIWELL *go downstairs.*)
(*Voice over*) Waiting for Miss Right, are we?
(ORTON *is still in the room.*)
(*Voice over*) Got a lovely skin, hasn't he? I like a nice skin.
(ORTON *sits on one of the beds. After a while* HALLIWELL
comes back and sits on the other.)

HALLIWELL: Well?

(ORTON *lies on his back on the bed and puts his hands behind
his head, looking at* HALLIWELL. HALLIWELL *is about to*

go to him when MRS SUGDEN *comes in with a tray and some hot drinks.*)

MRS SUGDEN: We were just having our hot drink.

(MR SUGDEN *comes in.*)

This is my hubby.

MR SUGDEN: You're older than him.

(HALLIWELL *shrugs.*)

MRS SUGDEN: Some people might take advantage.

MR SUGDEN: No. Women don't understand, do they? You're a lucky lad. Friend like this. Your own little flat. It's a real start in life.

EXT. BUILDING SITE. DAY. 1953

A street in Islington. The sound of distant church bells. Decorations. A dusty, half-naked young BRICKIE *is talking to* ORTON, *laughing.*

BRICKIE: Help yourself.

(ORTON *takes three or four bricks.*)

Here.

(*He piles about half a dozen bricks into* ORTON'S *arms, and watches him as he staggers away.*)

INT. ORTON AND HALLIWELL'S FLAT. HALLWAY. DAY. 1953

ORTON *nudges the door of the flat.* HALLIWELL *opens it.*

INT. ORTON AND HALLIWELL'S FLAT. DAY. 1953

HALLIWELL: Where did you get them?

ORTON: Nicked them while he wasn't looking.

(*He starts arranging the bricks against the wall with two planks across to make bookshelves.* HALLIWELL *is hanging a picture.* ORTON *opens a case and gets out a framed certificate and hangs that.* HALLIWELL *looks at it.*)

HALLIWELL: You can type?

ORTON: Forty words a minute. Neither of us seems to have any family photos.

HALLIWELL: I'm an orphan.

ORTON: I've always wanted to be an orphan. I could have been if it hadn't been for my parents.

HALLIWELL: My mother died when I was a boy. She was stung on the tongue by a wasp. One minute we were sitting down to breakfast, ten minutes later she was dead.

ORTON: That still leaves your dad.

HALLIWELL: Put his head in the gas oven when I was eighteen. Came down one morning, found him lying there. I switched the gas off, shaved, made a cup of tea and called the ambulance. In that order.

ORTON: I understand. My dad always took a back seat.

(HALLIWELL *gets out a pile of manuscripts.*)

HALLIWELL: My novels.

(ORTON *looks at them.*)

Anybody can act.

(ORTON *is obviously impressed. He looks at* HALLIWELL's *books as he helps to put them on the shelves.*)

ORTON: All these books. I'll never catch up.

HALLIWELL: I'm a cultivated person. You'll find it rubs off. Dictionary.

(*He hands* ORTON *the big two-volume* Oxford Dictionary.)

Can you spell?

ORTON: Yes. (*Pauses.*) But not accurately.

(*It is a conscious joke and they both laugh.* ORTON *gets some records and puts them on the lower shelves.*)

(*Confidingly.*) I don't understand Shakespeare.

HALLIWELL: We'll cross that bridge when we come to it.

(*He gets the TV set going and they settle down in front of it, as the Coronation Service starts. After a while* HALLIWELL *gets up and draws the curtains.*)

Improves the contrast.

(*They watch for a while then* HALLIWELL *puts his hand on* ORTON's *knee.*)

ORTON: This is a new experience for me.

(*Pause.*)

HALLIWELL: Yes?

ORTON: Television. I've never seen it before.

(HALLIWELL *goes on playing with* ORTON, *the scene played largely on* ORTON's *face with the Coronation Service over.*)

HALLIWELL: Do you like it?

ORTON: This?

HALLIWELL: Television.

> (ORTON *grins.* HALLIWELL *eases* ORTON'*s trousers down and off, with* ORTON *still seemingly glued to the screen, though lifting his legs to enable* HALLIWELL *to get his trousers off.* HALLIWELL *now has his arm around* ORTON, *who is sitting there in sweater, underpants, socks, but no trousers.*)

ORTON: It's the beginning of a new era.

> (*They get up.* HALLIWELL *goes into the bathroom.* ORTON *gets into bed.* HALLIWELL *is in the bathroom. The music is the build up to the beginning of* Zadok the Priest. HALLIWELL *gets into bed and they kiss. Cut to them lying happily in bed,* ORTON *cradled in* HALLIWELL'*s arms as the congregation on television in Westminster Abbey are heard singing 'All People That on Earth Do Dwell'.*)

INT. LEONIE ORTON'S HOUSE, LEICESTER.
THE PRESENT.

LEONIE, *her husband* GEORGE BARNETT, LAHR, ANTHEA (*now pregnant*). *The tape recorder is on. A* CHILD *plays under the table.*

LEONIE: Are you up here helping John?

ANTHEA: Holding his hand.

LAHR: Did Kenneth ever come up?

> (LEONIE *shakes her head.*)

Did you like him?

> (GEORGE *pulls a slight face.*)

LEONIE: I didn't dislike him. I could see what he saw in Joe after all. I couldn't see what Joe saw in him. Of course, I didn't know what went on.

GEORGE: (*To the* CHILD) Upstairs.

CHILD: Aww, Dad.

GEORGE: Upstairs.

> (*The* CHILD *goes.*)

LAHR: Did you know Joe was that way?

LEONIE: Yes.

GEORGE: You didn't.

LEONIE: I did and I didn't. The way you do, don't you? Mind

you, at our Douglas's wedding Mum caught him in bed with a bridesmaid.

GEORGE: So it's what I say. He can't have learned it in Leicester. He was corrupted.

LAHR: Joe wanted something from Kenneth. Kenneth wanted something from Joe. That's not corruption, it's collaboration.

LEONIE: He was born that way, or else it was my Mum.

ANTHEA: Women don't care anyway.

LEONIE: Taste of their own medicine.

(ANTHEA *and* LEONIE *giggle as* GEORGE *goes over to the door. The* CHILD *is just outside.*)

GEORGE: What did I say? Upstairs.

(*He closes the door and comes back.*)

LEONIE: The lavatories shocked me a bit. When I read his diary. But a boy stopped me the other day. 'I want to thank you for your brother's plays.' So what do you do?

GEORGE: Personally I think a lot of that's made up.

LEONIE: What?

GEORGE: The toilets. You have to go into all that, do you?

LEONIE: George.

GEORGE: Well, it all seems a bit unnecessary to me.

LEONIE: The lawnmower's not unnecessary. The Fiesta's not unnecessary. You want to be grateful we get the money from his plays.

GEORGE: Grateful? I work too, you know. This isn't royalties. This is plumbing money. He's nothing in Leicester, Joe Orton.

(*He goes out. Pause. The* CHILD *comes back into the room and sits on* LEONIE's *knee.*)

INT. ORTON AND HALLIWELL'S FLAT. NIGHT. 1953

ORTON: Ken.

HALLIWELL: What?

ORTON: You know you could be put in prison for this?

HALLIWELL: So could you.

ORTON: No. I'm the innocent party.

(ORTON *laughs in the dark.*)

34

INT. ORTON AND HALLIWELL'S FLAT. DAY. 1955
ORTON *and* HALLIWELL *are working side by side.* HALLIWELL
passes pages to ORTON. ORTON *makes notes on them, passes them
back.* HALLIWELL *laughs.* ORTON *gets bored. Stretches. Touches*
HALLIWELL.

HALLIWELL: No, I want to get on. Writing, John, is one-tenth
inspiration, nine-tenths perspiration.

ORTON: (*Chiming in*) Masturbation.

HALLIWELL: No.
(ORTON, *sulking, starts cutting up books.*)
That's a library book. You should respect books.

ORTON: I respect them more than you. You take them for
granted. (*He is angry.*) Oh shit. I'll never catch up.

HALLIWELL: (*Indicating the manuscript*) So? What's this? We're
halfway through a novel.

ORTON: You are, you mean.
(ORTON *lies on the bed with a book.* HALLIWELL *goes and
strokes him.*)

HALLIWELL: It's a collaboration. We've written this together.

ORTON: (*Sulkily*) Stop it. I'm reading.

HALLIWELL: You're not!

ORTON: Test me then.

HALLIWELL: (*Still stroking*) What on?

ORTON: Mythology.

HALLIWELL: Who was the father of Oedipus?

ORTON: Laius.

HALLIWELL: Who was his mother?

ORTON: Oh, fuck his mother.
(*Fade out and fade up to* ORTON *getting up from the bed in his
pants and sitting at the typewriter. The typing wakes*
HALLIWELL *who looks, smiles and goes back to sleep.*)

INT. FABER AND FABER BOARDROOM. DAY. 1956
HALLIWELL *and* ORTON *are talking to a* PUBLISHER, *sitting at
the boardroom table. The room is lined with books. Photos of Faber
authors. He has their manuscript in front of him.* HALLIWELL
concentrating on the PUBLISHER, ORTON *on his surroundings.*

PUBLISHER: *The Boy Hairdresser*. Nice title. Ye–es. I showed it
    to one or two . . . selected colleagues and we laughed.

HALLIWELL: You're kidding?

PUBLISHER: We had a real chuckle. The trouble is, normal sex is
    still a novelty for most people. In book form. A book such as
    yours which . . . very wittily . . .

HALLIWELL: We thought it was witty . . .

PUBLISHER: . . . explores the by-ways of sexuality . . . is . . .
    ahead of its time. We're a very conservative firm . . .
    (ORTON *has started to wander round the room. He looks at the*
    bookcase and while the PUBLISHER *is talking to* HALLIWELL
    slips an art book under his coat.)

HALLIWELL: Isn't one of the directors T. S. Eliot?
PUBLISHER: Yes. That's right.
HALLIWELL: Is he in the building?
PUBLISHER: Er . . . Thursday . . . yes, he is.
HALLIWELL: Fancy, John, we're under the same roof as
    T. S. Eliot.
    (ORTON *mutters to* HALLIWELL.)
    He wants to know which is his chair.
PUBLISHER: Er . . . that one.
    (ORTON *sits on it.* HALLIWELL *smiles indulgently from him to*
    the PUBLISHER, *who is now slightly alarmed by them. The*
    PUBLISHER *hands* HALLIWELL *his manuscript back.*)

Well, thank you for letting us see this.

HALLIWELL: You could keep it a bit longer if you want. Show it to a few more friends.

PUBLISHER: Thank you, no.

(*They are approaching the door.*)

HALLIWELL: And, remember, next time you run into Mr Eliot, tell him he's got two devoted fans in Islington who think *The Waste Land* is a real knock-out.

EXT. LONDON STREETS. DAY. 1956

ORTON *and* HALLIWELL *are walking away from Faber and Faber.* ORTON *is stowing away the book he has pinched in* HALLIWELL'*s ex-army pack.*

HALLIWELL: Never mind. At least you can say you've sat in the same chair as T. S. Eliot.

ORTON: Yes. I'm never going to wipe my bum again.

HALLIWELL: Why do you always leave the talking to me? It was your book as much as mine.

ORTON: I'm shy. It's not my territory.

(*A* YOUTH *is coming towards them.*)

Now this is dead centre me.

(*The* YOUTH *passes.*)

Nice bum.

HALLIWELL: He heard that.

ORTON: So what? Now *you're* shy.

(*They laugh and we should realize maybe for the first time why it is they are a good match. They walk along, eyeing the talent.*)

HALLIWELL: This is Mr Halliwell.

ORTON: Really? Doesn't knock on my box one bit. He's got a big one.

HALLIWELL: How do you know?

ORTON: Written all over his face.

(*They walk on. He sees another* YOUTH *coming.*)

Look at the package on this. He's lovely.

HALLIWELL: (*Frantically*) Where? Where?

ORTON: *Here.*

(*The* YOUTH *looks back.*)

We're on.

HALLIWELL: How? What did he do? I didn't see anything.

ORTON: What do you want, a telegram? Come on.

(*They follow. Fairly deserted streets.*)

He's built like a brick shithouse.

HALLIWELL: He's probably a policeman.

ORTON: I know. Isn't it wonderful?

HALLIWELL: Listen. We've got tickets to the Proms.

(*The* YOUTH *hesitates now and again, so that they catch up, then he is off again.* ORTON *is exhilarated.*)

ORTON: What's your name?

HALLIWELL: How do you mean, 'What's my name?'

ORTON: Mine's Kevin.

HALLIWELL: Mine's . . . Howard.

ORTON: Howard! That's a poncey name.

HALLIWELL: Patrick then.

ORTON: Oh. Catholic, are you? What do you do?

HALLIWELL: I don't know. What do you do?

ORTON: I'm a fitter. Car components.

HALLIWELL: I'm . . . a dog handler.

ORTON: On an individual basis, or are you a tool of a large organization?

HALLIWELL: I'm so shit scared, I don't know if I'll be able to do anything.

(ORTON *exhilarated and excited,* HALLIWELL *still quite worried.*)

We don't want to let this make us late for the Proms.

ORTON: Listen, sweetheart, which do you prefer, him or Sir Malcolm Sargent?

(*The* YOUTH *has gone into a doorway by a shop. The door closes.*)

INT. YOUTH'S HOUSE. DAY. 1956

ORTON *and* HALLIWELL *get to the door.* ORTON *pushes it slightly. It is open. They go up the stairs. A landing. Another door. Locked. They go up a further flight. A door ajar.* ORTON *pushes it slowly.*

INT. YOUTH'S HOUSE: HIS ROOM. DAY. 1956

ORTON *goes in first. The* YOUTH *is standing in the middle of the room.* HALLIWELL *knocks before coming in and when he does come in it is with a kind of social smile on his face.* ORTON, *on the other hand, stands square in front of the* YOUTH, *saying nothing.*

ORTON: Hello, my name's Kevin.

YOUTH: Mine's Kenneth.

HALLIWELL: Oh. Mine's Kenneth too!

ORTON: Oh shit!

HALLIWELL: (*Hurriedly*) Only my friends call me Patrick.

YOUTH: We're all friends here.

(ORTON *slowly undoes the* YOUTH's *shirt.*)

ORTON: Do you kiss?

(*The* YOUTH *nods.* ORTON *kisses him.* HALLIWELL *watches.* ORTON *then turns and kisses* HALLIWELL.)

HALLIWELL: (*Whispering to* ORTON) I don't think he likes me.

ORTON: (*To* YOUTH) You like him, don't you?

YOUTH: Sure.

ORTON: Kiss him!

(*The* YOUTH *does so.* ORTON *watches them both with a kind of triumph on his face.*)

INT. ORTON AND HALLIWELL'S FLAT. NIGHT. 1956
Tranquil scene with them both in the flat at Noel Road – where the collage has begun to spread further round the walls and the book ORTON *has stolen lies open with an illustration cut out. Working and listening to music on the record player. The collage spreads round the room as* PEGGY *speaks.*

PEGGY: (*Voice over*) And so ten years passed.

LAHR: (*Voice over*) Not like that?

PEGGY: (*Voice over*) No, silly. Though quite like that. Nothing happened. Looking back on it I suppose it was some kind of preparation.

LAHR: (*Voice over*) An education maybe.

PEGGY: (*Voice over*) Well, if it seemed like that to Joe, it can't have done to Ken.

LAHR: (*Voice over*) No.

PEGGY: (*Voice over*) His hair was falling out.

LAHR: (*Voice over*) Oh God! I know the feeling.

PEGGY: (*Voice over*) And whereas he had stopped writing, Joe

40

had started. But still they were both failures, so it didn't
matter.
LAHR: (*Voice over*) It didn't matter yet.
PEGGY: (*Voice over*) Quite.

INT. ORTON AND HALLIWELL'S FLAT.
DAY/DUSK. 1962
The walls are three-quarters covered in collage. HALLIWELL *cuts a
picture out of a library book and tries to find a place for it on the wall.*
ORTON *is reading.* HALLIWELL *goes into the kitchen, the camera
staying with* ORTON, *placidly reading.*
HALLIWELL: (*Out of shot*) Do you want rice pudding with the
sardines or separate?
ORTON: With.
HALLIWELL: (*Out of shot*) Jam?
(HALLIWELL *is in the kitchen, poised with jam.*)
ORTON: (*Voice over*) No.
(HALLIWELL *puts jam on his own plate of sardines and rice
pudding, but not on Orton's. He carries the food in.* ORTON *eats
his while reading.* HALLIWELL *sits on the bed eating his.*
ORTON *stops and looks out of the window.*)
Mozart was dead by the time he was my age. I'm not even
young any more.
HALLIWELL: What about me?
ORTON: You never were.
(*He carefully sticks a piece of paper on the dust-cover of a library
book.*)
I can't see how we're ever going to make our mark defacing
library books.
(*He props up the library book on his desk. It is a biography of
Sybil Thorndyke now adorned with a picture of a Stone Age
woman with large tits.*)

INT. ISLINGTON PUBLIC LIBRARY. DAY. 1962
Cut to a library date stamp coming down hard in a book. ORTON *and*
HALLIWELL *have just had their books stamped and are going out.
The assistant,* MISS BATTERSBY, *looks after them suspiciously, as
does* MR CUNLIFFE, *the librarian.*

CUNLIFFE: You didn't tell me one of them was a nancy.

MISS BATTERSBY: I'm sorry, Mr Cunliffe?

CUNLIFFE: The bald one, Miss Battersby. A homosexual. A shirt-lifter.

MISS BATTERSBY: In Islington?

CUNLIFFE: Haven't you noticed? Large areas of the borough are being restored and painted Thames Green.
(CUNLIFFE *is looking at their address on the library tickets.*)
Noel Road. This calls for a little detective work, Miss Battersby.

EXT. NOEL ROAD. DAY. 1962
CUNLIFFE *is standing outside Noel Road, looking up at number 25. Faint sounds of typing from upstairs.* CUNLIFFE *looks up and walks on. There is a wrecked car further down the street. He stops by it as voice-over begins, accompanied by a typewriter.*

INT. CUNLIFFE'S OFFICE. DAY. 1962
An office, glass-panelled, overlooking the library's stacked shelves.
CUNLIFFE: (*Dictating to* MISS BATTERSBY . . .) Registration KYR 450. The above-mentioned vehicle appears to be derelict and abandoned in Noel Road and I have been given to understand that you are the owner thereof.
(*Mix through to:*)

INT. ORTON AND HALLIWELL'S FLAT. DAY. 1962
HALLIWELL *is reading the same letter.*
HALLIWELL: '. . . but before enforcing remedies I give you the opportunity to remove the vehicle from the highway.' The little prick. Standard Vanguard indeed. Seat yourself at our trusty Remington, John, and we will piss on this person from a great height.
(ORTON *sits at the typewriter.*)
(*Dictating*) 'Thank you for your dreary little letter.'

ORTON: Dismal's better.

HALLIWELL: Dismal then. 'I should like to know who provided you with this mysterious information . . .'

ORTON: Furnished is better than provided. More municipal in
tone.
HALLIWELL: 'As I have never possessed a car of any make
whatsoever.'

INT. CUNLIFFE'S OFFICE. DAY. 1962
*A magnifying glass examining two specimens of typing. We come out
slightly to see it is the letter* HALLIWELL *has sent being compared
with one of the book jackets we have seen* ORTON *doctoring. Other
doctored books lie on the table, some with outrageous covers, including
one of the* Collected Poems *of John Betjeman illustrated by a picture
of a nude old man, tattooed from head to foot.*
CUNLIFFE: (*Voice over, the magnifying glass looking at the book
jacket*) You will note that the typing, Miss Battersby, is the
same. Our book jacket! Their letter! Got you my beauties!
'Fucked by Monty' indeed. Men died, Miss Battersby. Died.

INT. POLICE COURT. DAY. 1962
Islington Magistrates Court. ORTON *and* HALLIWELL *are in the
dock.*
COUNSEL: Exhibit 7.
(*The* CLERK *hands him Exhibit 7.*)
This is the novel *Clouds of Witness* by the noted authoress,
Dorothy L. Sayers. Can you read what you found on the
back of the jacket?
(*As the* POLICEMAN *reads, the camera takes in the various
people in the court. The thinly attended gallery, a* WOMAN
eating a sandwich, MRS SUGDEN, CUNLIFFE *looking
pleased with himself.*)
POLICEMAN: 'When little Betty Macdree says she has been
interfered with her mother first laughs. It is only something
the kiddy has picked up off the television. But when sorting
through the laundry, Mrs Macdree discovers a new pair of
knickers are missing, she thinks again. Her mother takes
little Betty to the police station where, to everyone's
surprise, she identifies PC Brenda Coolidge as her attacker.
A search is made of the Women's Police Barracks. What is
found there is a seven-inch phallus and a pair of knickers

43

of the type worn by Betty. All looks black for kindly PC Coolidge. This is one of the most enthralling stories ever written by Miss Sayers. Read it behind closed doors. And have a good shit while you're reading it.'

INT. POLICE COURT. DAY. 1962
MAGISTRATE: The Probation Officer has suggested you are both frustrated authors. Well, if you're so clever at making fun of what more talented people have written you should have a shot at writing books yourselves. You won't find that such a pushover. Sheer malice and destruction, the pair of you. I sentence you both to six months.

44

ORTON: Both? Fucking Ada!
HALLIWELL: It was your idea.
ORTON: But I'm the youngest.

EXT. OPEN PRISON. DAY. 1962
ORTON, *stripped to the waist, exercises with the weights on a lawn in
the sunshine.*)
PEGGY: (*Voice over*) Prison worked wonders for Joe. Made a man
of him if you like. And being a man, of course, he made out
of it much more of an ordeal than in fact it was.
LAHR: (*Voice over*) Where did he go?
PEGGY: (*Voice over*) Brixton, for about five minutes. Then one of
those open places in Sussex. Quite near my health farm
actually, and with much the same effect.
LAHR: (*Voice over*) Though at rather less expense.
PEGGY: (*Voice over*) Yes.

INT. PRISON PSYCHIATRIST'S OFFICE. DAY. 1962
PSYCHIATRIST: What about your parents?
ORTON: Dead. Both of them, when I was a little kiddy. I'm an
orphan. The guy I share a room with, Ken, he cracks on he's
the orphan. Don't you believe it. Reckons he got up one
morning and found his dad with his head in the gas oven and
didn't even call an ambulance. How is he by the way?
(*The* PSYCHIATRIST *nods.*)

INT. PRISON PSYCHIATRIST'S OFFICE. DAY. 1962
The sound of HALLIWELL *weeping out of shot.*
PSYCHIATRIST: Well, that was your mother. Tell me about
your father.
(HALLIWELL *blows his nose.*)
HALLIWELL: Nothing to tell. I was eighteen. Came down one
morning and found him with his head in the gas oven.
PSYCHIATRIST: You called the ambulance, naturally?
HALLIWELL: Eventually. I made a cup of tea first. Well, he was
quite plainly dead.
PSYCHIATRIST: You weren't fond of him?
HALLIWELL: Not particularly.

PSYCHIATRIST: You're fond of your room-mate?
HALLIWELL: We're everything to one another.
PSYCHIATRIST: Sleep together, do you?
HALLIWELL: No, but we have sex.
    (PSYCHIATRIST *smiles patiently*.)
PSYCHIATRIST: Are you sure?
HALLIWELL: Yes.
PSYCHIATRIST: You don't mean you *want* to have sex?
HALLIWELL: No, we do.
PSYCHIATRIST: But your friend's not like that, is he? He's
    married. He's got a child. You seem surprised. Are you?
HALLIWELL: Not really.
PSYCHIATRIST: Besides, your friend's much younger than you.

INT. PRISON: CORRIDOR. DAY. 1962
The PSYCHIATRIST *strolls with* ORTON *down the corridor, back
towards Orton's room.*
PSYCHIATRIST: This may come as a shock to you, but I suspect
    your friend may be . . . homosexual.
ORTON: Jesus. And there I am sleeping in the same room with
    him.
PSYCHIATRIST: You mentioned your wife. Where is she now?
ORTON: Last time I heard she'd taken the kiddy to Lyme Regis.
PSYCHIATRIST: Try and team up with them again. Make a fresh
    start.
ORTON: Don't you worry.
    (*They have come to the door of Orton's room.*)
PSYCHIATRIST: Not too spartan, is it?
ORTON: On the contrary. A room of one's own.
    (*He enters the room.*)

INT. PRISON: ORTON'S ROOM. DAY. 1962
ORTON *lies down on the bed, smiling. He takes up a pad and starts
writing.*
PEGGY: (*Voice over*) Prison gives a writer credentials.
LAHR: (*Voice over*) For everyone else it takes them away.
PEGGY: (*Voice over*) It was the first time in ten years they'd been
    split up.

LAHR: (*Voice over*) So prison was a taste of freedom.
PEGGY: (*Voice over*) For Joe.

INT. ORTON AND HALLIWELL'S FLAT. DAY. 1963
ORTON *takes the cover off his typewriter and begins to copy something out.*
HALLIWELL: I can't stand you typing. It's a dead end; we're going to have to forget all that.
ORTON: Why don't you go dangle your flaccid tool over the windowsill. Some casual passer-by might give it a pull. I'm working.
HALLIWELL: (*Shouting at* ORTON'*s back*) Working? This doesn't bring anything in. It never has. We owe money. We want jobs. Proper jobs. Work nine to five. It's time we joined the human race.
(ORTON *is typing with a set face.*)
ORTON: You can. I'm not.
(HALLIWELL *starts reading over his shoulder.*)
HALLIWELL: When did you do this? I haven't seen this.
ORTON: It's a radio play. I did it on my own. In prison. I've sent it to the BBC.
HALLIWELL: Why didn't you tell me? I could have helped you write a proper letter. You'll never hear back.
ORTON: (*Indicating the letter*) I already have.
(HALLIWELL *reads and* ORTON *begins weightlifting.*
HALLIWELL *starts to read aloud.*)
HALLIWELL: 'We had a little room. And our life was made quite comfortable by the National Assistance Board. We had a lot of friends. All creeds and colours. No circumstances at all. We were happy enough. We were young.'

INT. BBC STUDIO. DAY. 1963
ACTORS *in front of microphone.*
ACTOR 1: I was seventeen. He was twenty-three. You can't do better for yourself than that, can you? We were bosom friends. I hope I haven't shocked you.
ACTOR 2: As close as that?
ACTOR 1: We had separate beds. He was a stickler for convention.

47

INT. BBC STUDIO: PRODUCER'S BOX. DAY. 1963
HALLIWELL, ORTON *and the* PRODUCER *are listening*.

ACTOR 1: (*Voice over*) But we spent every night in each other's
   company. It was the reason we never got any work done.
   (ORTON *laughs*.)
   (*Voice over*) I used to base my life round him. You don't
   often get that, do you?

ACTOR 2: (*Voice over*) No.
   (*We see* HALLIWELL *listening*.)

ACTOR 1: (*Voice over*) He had personality. That indefinable
   something.

48

INT. PEGGY RAMSAY'S OFFICE: PASSAGEWAY.
DAY. 1964
ORTON *is going down the passage to Peggy's office with voice-over of*
ACTOR I *continuing.*
ACTOR I: (*Voice over*) His mentality wasn't fully developed, but
he was bound to make good sooner or later. He was the go-
ahead type.
(ORTON *opens the door marked* MARGARET RAMSAY
PLAY AGENT. *He goes in.*)

INT. PEGGY RAMSAY'S OFFICE. DAY. 1964
PEGGY's *voice is heard, as in the earlier scene.*
PEGGY: (*Voice over*) I knew nothing about him when he walked
in. He had considerable confidence and charm. I thought the
radio play was derivative. I said so: he didn't mind.
ORTON: I'm writing a better one. For the stage.
PEGGY: Well, Mr Orton, that sounds gorgeous. Would it be very
rude to inquire how you are managing to live?
ORTON: National Assistance. Three pounds ten a week. I've just
come out of gaol.
(PEGGY *roots in her handbag.*)
PEGGY: Excellent. The papers love all that. Now this is what we
call an advance. It means that when you finish this new play
you're writing, the one that's going to be better, you bring it
along and show me.
(*She gives* ORTON *a bundle of pound notes.*)
John Orton. (*Frowns.*) Don't like that. Sounds too much like
John Osborne. Are you attached to John? As a name? No?
Then try to think of another, dear.
(ORTON *is leaving.*)
ORTON: Next time . . .
(*She looks up.*)
Next time I come can I bring my friend?

INT. ARTS THEATRE: STALLS. DAY. 1964
A rehearsal of Entertaining Mr Sloane *is in progress.* ORTON *is in
the stalls and* HALLIWELL *in the circle. The* DIRECTOR *plots some
stage business with two of the actors. One of them is in his underpants.*

49

DIRECTOR: Now is that better? Joe?
ORTON: Fine.
> (*He is writing on a pad on his knee.*)
DIRECTOR: It feels better to me. Does it feel better to you?
ACTOR 1: It's better for me.
ACTOR 2: Better for me too.
DIRECTOR: Success!
> (*The* ACTORS *smile. An atmosphere of relief.*)
HALLIWELL: Except that it's not our play.
> (ORTON *is expressionless.*)
> You're making it into a cheap sex farce. That's not what we
> wrote.
> (ORTON *says nothing.*)
DIRECTOR: We?
ORTON: Ken thinks . . .
DIRECTOR: Listen. You wrote the play. I'm directing it. I don't
care a damn what this refugee from a second-hand clothes
shop thinks.
> (HALLIWELL *leaves and we hear the swing doors flapping
> behind him.*)
> I won't have him at rehearsals. It fucks up the actors. After
> all, it's your play. It *is* your play, isn't it?
ORTON: Of course it is.
> (ORTON *gets up to go.*)
DIRECTOR: Then what's all this 'we'?

INT. ARTS THEATRE: FOYER. DAY. 1964
ORTON *goes into the foyer and sits down still studying his pad.
A* CHARWOMAN *mops the floor expressionlessly, while this is going on.*
HALLIWELL: You just want to be liked, that's your trouble.
ORTON: Am I twenty-five or twenty-six?
> (ORTON *is writing on a pad.*)
> For publicity purposes. Peggy is pestering me for some
> undisputed facts.
HALLIWELL: Why not tell the truth? Thirty-one.
ORTON: I can't put thirty-one. I don't look thirty-one. Besides
thirty-one is a well-known bus. Married or single?
> (*Silence.*)

Married and divorced. One kiddy. Look.
(*He shows* HALLIWELL *the manuscript.*)
I've dedicated it to you. What more do you want?
(HALLIWELL *looks at the dedication.*)
HALLIWELL: Could you put my full name? Not just Kenneth.
(ORTON *shrugs.*)
ORTON: I'll put your phone number too if you want.

INT. WIGMAKER'S SHOP. DAY. 1964
A cubicle. HALLIWELL'*s head is being measured by a* WIGMAKER.
ORTON *sits watching. The* WIGMAKER *goes out.*
HALLIWELL: Why now? You're not ashamed of me?
(ORTON *shakes his head as the* WIGMAKER *returns with one or
two wigs, which* HALLIWELL *tries on, with* ORTON *watching
critically.*)
ORTON: Hair loss is often thought of as a sign of sexual potency.
Does your experience bear that out?
WIGMAKER: More people wear wigs than is commonly
realized: trades union leaders, sporting personalities,
members of the Royal Family.
ORTON: It's better than the beret.
(HALLIWELL *is obviously taken with it.*)
WIGMAKER: Shall we keep it on?
HALLIWELL: Oh yes. I think so. I shall wear it to our first night.
(*He is obviously very pleased, and* ORTON *is pleased that he is
pleased.*)
WIGMAKER: That will be seventy pounds.
HALLIWELL: Seventy pounds!
ORTON: This is on me.
HALLIWELL: And this is on me.
(*He looks at himself in the wig.*)

EXT. ARTS THEATRE. NIGHT. 1964
Neon sign: ENTERTAINING MR SLOANE BY JOE ORTON.
ORTON *and* HALLIWELL *looking at it.*
HALLIWELL: I'm not calling you Joe. You sound like rough
trade. To me you're John. You'll always be John.
(ORTON *puts his arm round* HALLIWELL'*s neck.*)

ORTON: For Ken and Joe. Opportunity Knocks.

INT. ARTS THEATRE: DRESSING ROOM. NIGHT. 1964
Over the tannoy the sound of the last scene of Sloane, *punctuated by laughter. An* OLD WAITRESS *from the theatre arranges glasses on the dressing-room table. Bottles of champagne, telegrams, etc. Applause starts, tumultuously. She betrays no sign of emotion or expectation, merely opens the door and waits outside in the corridor.*

INT. ARTS THEATRE: BACKSTAGE. NIGHT. 1964
Later in the corridor. The party is in full swing. It has spilled out into the corridor and ORTON *fights his way out of the room, glass in hand.* ORTON *straightens* HALLIWELL's *wig and pulls him out of the room.*
PARTY-GOERS: (*Out of vision*) Joe, Joe!
ORTON: I won't be long.
HALLIWELL: I was enjoying myself. Where are we going?

EXT. GENTS' LAVATORY. NIGHT. 1964
ORTON *and* HALLIWELL *walking along by a park.*
HALLIWELL: Where're we going? What about the party?
    (*They are approaching a gents' lavatory.*)
ORTON: I just want to see if it works.
HALLIWELL: What?
ORTON: The wig.
HALLIWELL: No, no. Please, Joe. I don't want to.
ORTON: Stand there.
    (*He leaves* HALLIWELL *standing uneasily outside the lavatory.* ORTON *withdraws and sits on a seat.* HALLIWELL's *hand keeps straying nervously to his wig.* ORTON *smiles reassuringly. Unseen by* HALLIWELL, *a* YOUTH *comes up to* ORTON.)
YOUTH: You got the time?
ORTON: Not right now. (*Pause.*) See the fellow in the wig? He's wanting it. Ask him.
YOUTH: No fear.
ORTON: Go on.
    (*He slips the* YOUTH *a quid. The* YOUTH *goes up to* HALLIWELL, *pretty insolently.*)

YOUTH: You got a match?

HALLIWELL: What?

YOUTH: A light?

HALLIWELL: I've just stopped smoking as a matter of fact.

YOUTH: Pity. I was thinking of popping in for a jimmy riddle. You know.

(*The* YOUTH *goes into the lavatory.* HALLIWELL *rushes over to* ORTON.)

HALLIWELL: It works. It really works.

ORTON: Go on then. Get in there.

HALLIWELL: I daren't.

ORTON: Do you want me to come in?

HALLIWELL: No. No.

(*He adjusts his wig and goes in, leaving* ORTON *on the seat. A* MAN *comes up and sits beside him. Behind them we see either* TWO POLICEMEN *approaching, or the flashing blue light of a police car.*)

MAN: You don't want it stuck up your arse by any chance?

ORTON: If you mean what I think you mean, no.

(MAN *gets up.*)

MAN: No harm in asking. Hey up.

(ORTON *looks round and sees the police car or the* POLICEMEN. *He gets up very quickly and rushes into the lav.*)

INT. GENTS' LAVATORY. NIGHT. 1964

The lav seems to be empty.

ORTON: Ken, Ken! Where are you for Christ's sake?

(*A cubicle door opens. He is there with the* YOUTH, *but plainly nothing has happened.*)

HALLIWELL: We were just having a chat.

ORTON: Police. Out. Quick.

YOUTH: Jesus.

(*There are two entrances to the lav.* ORTON *and* HALLIWELL *run out of one and a moment or two later the* POLICEMEN *come in at the other as the* YOUTH *stands in a stall. One stands behind the* YOUTH *while the other pushes open the doors of the cubicle. The* YOUTH *zips up his flies.*)

A piss is as good as a pint. Night all.

53

EXT. STREET. NIGHT. 1964
Cut to ORTON *and* HALLIWELL *running.* HALLIWELL *takes off
his wig to run more easily. They eventually slow down.* HALLIWELL
*puts on his wig again. They have come back to the Arts Theatre. They
look up at the neon sign 'Entertaining Mr Sloane' Written by Joe Orton.)*
HALLIWELL: Thank you.
ORTON: Thank *you.*
  (*He checks no one is looking then kisses him.*)

INT. ORTON AND HALLIWELL'S FLAT. DAY. 1967
ORTON *is sitting at his desk, above which is a collage made by*
HALLIWELL *of the notices and comments on* Loot.
ORTON: My second play *Loot* is a bigger hit than my first. It's
  also a better play. And it is the critics' choice: Best play of
  the year. The film rights have been sold for a record figure.
  Currently I am working on a screenplay for four boys who
  are nudging Jesus Christ for position of Number One Most
  Famous Person Ever. But have I met these fabled creatures?
  Have I met their manager, Miss Brian Epstein? Have I been
  paid? No. They why am I doing it?
HALLIWELL: Vanity.
ORTON: Answer supplied by the envious queen with whom I
  share what is laughably called my life. Well, I'm going to
  jack it in, Beatles or no Beatles. What I would like to do at
  this moment would be to ease down their Liverpudlian
  underpants and ram my Remington up their arses. The
  lovable mopheads.
HALLIWELL: What about me?
ORTON: What about you?
HALLIWELL: I can't remember when you last touched my cock.
  Well, I can actually, it was about two years ago, only I don't
  know the actual date. Pity. If you'd said, 'Ken, this is the last
  time I'm going to touch your cock', I could've done
  something to mark the occasion. Cracked a bottle of
  champagne, maybe, or put in my diary 'The last time Joe
  touched my cock. Grouse shooting begins'.
ORTON: Maybe we should go away. Somewhere there's plenty of
  sex. And I don't mean Southport. Somewhere even you

54

might be happy. Morocco maybe. What do you think?

HALLIWELL: I don't want to go away. I just want to go to the awards. I could. Look. (*Shows him the invitation*) 'Joe Orton and Guest'. I'd behave. I wouldn't say a word. Promise.

ORTON: No.

HALLIWELL: Why?

ORTON: Because it's for me. I wrote it.

HALLIWELL: I gave you the title.

ORTON: OK. So when they have awards for titles you can go to that.

(HALLIWELL *launches himself at* ORTON *with a carving knife.*)

Jesus!

(*They wrestle. The telephone rings.*)

HALLIWELL: Yes? No. This is Mr Orton's personal assistant. No. He's tied up at this moment. (*His tone changes.*) Oh, I see. Yes. Yes. Thank you. (*To* ORTON) Paul McCartney is calling to see you. He's on his way now.

ORTON: Here?

(HALLIWELL *nods.*)

Shit!

(*He immediately starts taking off his clothes.* HALLIWELL *immediately starts tidying the flat. Both rushing around,* ORTON *changing,* HALLIWELL *tidying, and having this conversation.*)

Was that him?

HALLIWELL: No. Someone more cultured. The chauffeur I think.

ORTON: Did you tell him the address?

HALLIWELL: He knew the address. I wish I'd known. The place is a pigsty.

ORTON: He won't mind. He's used to it. He's an ordinary working-class boy. They all are.

HALLIWELL: (*Putting on some make-up*) He's the nicest though. I've always liked him. The others are more . . . instinctive. I won't stop. Just introduce me and say whom I am then I'll make myself scarce.

(*They are now sitting side by side on one of the beds, waiting. There is the sound of a car door slamming.*)

This is what it must feel like when one's about to meet the
Queen.

ORTON: Except when one meets the Queen one normally hasn't
just threatened to ram a typewriter up her arse.
(*The bell rings downstairs.* ORTON *jerks his head for*
HALLIWELL *to answer.* HALLIWELL *goes out, leaving*
ORTON *sitting on the bed.*)

INT. ORTON AND HALLIWELL'S FLAT: DOWNSTAIRS.
DAY. 1967
HALLIWELL *opens the door.*
CHAUFFEUR: Mr Orton?
HALLIWELL: I'm his personal assistant.
(*He glances over the* CHAUFFEUR'S *shoulder at the waiting
Rolls.*)

INT. ORTON AND HALLIWELL'S ROOM. DAY. 1967
ORTON *sitting on the bed. Sound of* HALLIWELL *running up the
stairs.*
HALLIWELL: He's waiting for you in the car.
(ORTON *goes out leaving* HALLIWELL.)

EXT. NOEL ROAD. DAY. 1967
The CHAUFFEUR *opens the door.* ORTON *gets in and closes the
door. The* CHAUFFEUR *goes round and is about to start when*
HALLIWELL *runs out of the house with the script. He bangs on the
window.*
HALLIWELL: Joe.
(*The window slides down and* ORTON *takes it, maybe with a
wink.* HALLIWELL *gazes after the car as it drives off.*)
That was Paul McCartney.
MRS SUGDEN: Was it? Oh Kenneth, you are going to have some
memories.

INT. ORTON AND HALLIWELL'S FLAT. DAY. 1967
HALLIWELL *enters the flat and begins to look for the remainder of
his pills. We see him put the awards ceremony invitation card back on
the table as* PEGGY'S *voice-over begins.*

INT. DORCHESTER HOTEL: AWARDS CEREMONY.
NIGHT. 1967
We see PEGGY *sitting next to* ORTON *at a table, as the* AWARDS
CHAIRMAN *begins his presentation.*
PEGGY: (*Voice over*) So Ken didn't get to the Awards and I did.
At moments of triumph men can do without their wives.
LAHR: (*Voice over*) They cramp our style.
PEGGY: (*Voice over*) But sharing is what wives want.
LAHR: (*Voice over*) Right. And Ken was a coach as well as a wife.
PEGGY: (*Voice over*) Poor Ken. Still it was a popular win. Joe was
young. The play was naughty. It all seemed very bold.
ORTON: My plays are about getting away with it. And the ones
who get away with it are the guilty. It's the innocent who get
it in the neck. That all seems pretty true to life to me. Not a
fantasy at all. I've got away with it so far. And I'm going to
go on.

INT. DORCHESTER HOTEL CLOAKROOM. NIGHT. 1967
A few GUESTS *from the dinner mill around. Outside the cloakroom*
ORTON *is handed his fur coat.*
PEGGY: Can I drop you?
ORTON: Actually the twenty-four's handier.
PEGGY: Why, where are you going?
ORTON: (*Giving her a kiss*) Just going on somewhere.

EXT. GENTS' LAVATORY, HOLLOWAY ROAD.
NIGHT. 1967
ORTON *is carrying the award in a plastic carrier bag. He goes down
the steps into the gents' lav.*

INT. GENTS' LAVATORY, HOLLOWAY ROAD.
NIGHT. 1967
Standing on the steps, his head level with the top step, is an OLD
MAN. *As* ORTON *goes by, the* OLD MAN *coughs, loudly.* ORTON
goes along a short tiled passage into a dimly lit lav. One MAN *is
pissing in a stall.* ORTON *stands in the next but one stall to him and
takes out his cock. The* MAN *looks, then edges back slightly showing
his.* ORTON *has put the bag with the* Evening Standard *award down*

by his feet. It is a statuette of an impassive bronze woman.

ORTON *goes over to the bulb holder, removing the bulb. This leaves the gents' lit only by light spilling in from the street.* FIGURES *can be seen in silhouette. Light sometimes falls on flesh or underwear.*

ORTON *goes up to the* MAN *and puts his hand down to his cock. The door of one of the cubicles opens and another* MAN *is there. He comes out, loosens* ORTON'S *trousers and feels his bum. There is a cough.*

Everyone bags a stall as a YOUTH *in black leather comes in, pisses then goes. By which time everybody is at it again.*

Another MAN *comes in and watches what is going on. There are about seven or eight* MEN *in the toilet in all.*

Someone is sucking ORTON'S *cock. He comes. Zips up his fly. Does a farewell tour of the toilet.*

Goes down the cubicles to where one MAN *is kneeling on the floor, his face pressed to the partition. On the other side of the partition another* MAN *is pressed up against the partition, his cock presumably through a hole in the partition in the other* MAN'S *mouth. As* ORTON *looks at this spectacle, the* MAN *doing the sucking turns and looks mutely up at* ORTON.

ORTON *goes.*

INT. ORTON AND HALLIWELL'S FLAT. NIGHT. 1967
ORTON *typing.*
HALLIWELL: What did you say? Did you say anything?
ORTON: Nothing. You know me. 'Thank you.' Various people kissed me.
  (*It seems he is talking about the lavatory, but as we see*
  HALLIWELL *looking at the award, we realize he is talking about the dinner.* HALLIWELL *runs his finger over Orton's name on the award.*)
HALLIWELL: You should pack.
  (ORTON *is finishing typing and taking the paper out of the typewriter and putting it in a looseleaf folder, which forms his diary.*)
ORTON: Do you read my diary?
HALLIWELL: No. Why?
ORTON: It puts things in perspective. (*Pause.*) Should I take my typewriter?

HALLIWELL: No. This is a holiday.
ORTON: Just in case.

EXT. STREET, TANGIER. DAY. 1967
A long row of ARAB BOYS *sitting smiling on a wall. Their heads all turn as* ORTON *and* HALLIWELL *pass.* TWO ARAB BOYS *help them with their suitcases.* ORTON *and* HALLIWELL *walk along with them, obviously very pleased with this state of affairs,* HALLIWELL *particularly. They knock at the door of a house. Another smiling* BOY *opens it.*

59

INT. APARTMENT, TANGIER. DAY. 1967
ORTON *and* HALLIWELL *are shown round the apartment by the*
three smiling BOYS. *Particularly the bath and the shower and the*
beds. All the BOYS *sit on the beds and bounce up and down, laughing*
a lot.

EXT. THE BEACH, TANGIER. DAY. 1967
More BOYS *running across the sands, this time with* ORTON *and*
HALLIWELL, *splashing, etc., in the sea. The music is 'By the Sea,*
By the Sea, By the Beautiful Sea' as in Some Like It Hot.

INT. APARTMENT, TANGIER. DAY. 1967
Music suddenly stops and ORTON *and* HALLIWELL *are sitting*
across the kitchen table opposite two of the BOYS.
ORTON: Which do you want . . . Abbott or Costello?
HALLIWELL: Which do you think likes me?
ORTON: I'm not sure liking comes into it.
    (*He takes* BOY I *on to the balcony. They stand there, looking*
    at the view, as ORTON *runs his hand down the* BOY'*s back. The*
    BOY *smiles.* ORTON *sits on the parapet looking into the kitchen*
    where HALLIWELL *is getting nowhere.*)
HALLIWELL: And you say your brother's in Epsom?
BOY 2: Epsom. Yes.
HALLIWELL: Working in a hotel?
BOY 2: Yes. Waiter.
HALLIWELL: Epsom's in Surrey. Near London.
BOY 2: London. Yes.
    (BOY 2 *yawns.* ORTON *nudges* BOY I *who goes into the*
    kitchen and says something to BOY 2 *in Arabic.* BOY 2
    instantly gets up and puts his hands around HALLIWELL'*s*
    neck. They get up and go into one of the bedrooms. BOY 2 *leads.*)

INT. APARTMENT, TANGIER: HALLIWELL'S
BEDROOM. DAY. 1967
BOY 2 *making love to* HALLIWELL. HALLIWELL *is trying to*
keep his wig on. BOY 2 *smiles. Reaches out and takes it off.*
HALLIWELL *stops him.* BOY 2 *smiles. Pushes his hand away.*
Takes off the wig and puts it by the bed and smiles. HALLIWELL *smiles.*

INT. APARTMENT, TANGIER. DAY. 1967
ORTON *and* HALLIWELL *are in bed with the two Arab* BOYS.
A joint is circulating.
ORTON: And to think there's another two coming round at
    seven. My life is beginning to run to a timetable no member
    of the Royal Family would tolerate.
HALLIWELL: I'm improving.
ORTON: You are. Having your dick sucked regularly is turning
    you back into a human being.
    (*The phone rings.*)

61

HALLIWELL: Who's this? Nobody knows we're here.

ORTON: I gave the Beatles' office the number just in case. It's Brian Epstein.

(*Cut to* EPSTEIN, *then cut between the two.* EPSTEIN *is looking through the script.*)

EPSTEIN: I was very impressed with your screenplay, Joe. Some areas I'm not sure I've understood correctly and perhaps you could talk me through those?

ORTON: Delighted.

EPSTEIN: Yes. (*Looking through the script*) Now the Beatles are all pursuing the same girl, right?

ORTON: Yes.

EPSTEIN: We–ell, maybe. Knowing the boys as I do I'd say that was . . . well . . . iffy. However it's on page fifty-three, scene eighty-six we definitely seem to kiss reality goodbye. 'Cut to the boys in bed with Susan. One of them is smoking a joint. He passes it round.' Two points there, Joe. One: these boys do not take drugs. They never have taken drugs. They never will take drugs.

ORTON: It's only a joint.

EPSTEIN: (*Ignoring this*) Second point: if the boys are all in bed with Susan this means, as I understand it, they are all in bed with each other. No, no, no. No, no. NO.

(*He forces a laugh.*)

ORTON: (*Innocently*) Why?

EPSTEIN: Why? Because these are normal healthy boys.

ORTON: I take it they do sleep together?

EPSTEIN: They do not.

ORTON: They are all very pretty. I imagined they just had a good time. Sang and smoked and fucked everything in sight including each other. I thought that was what success meant.

EPSTEIN: Mr Orton. Success means . . . well, it means a respect for the public. Besides, one of the boys is happily married. I'm sorry, Mr Orton. I hope you are having a pleasant vacation.

ORTON: You bet we are.

INT/EXT. TANGIER: MONTAGE. 1967
ORTON *and* HALLIWELL *lying on rocks, sunning themselves like lizards.*

MOROCCAN BOYS *showering against the white stucco outside wall of a beach house.* ORTON *showers with them.*

Rubbing oil on BOY's *back, hand under bathing suit.*

ORTON *hosing down the lush foliage on the patio, turning the hose on the* BOYS.

Coming out of the water. Rolling in the hot sand. Muddy and happy. Baking in the sun.

Sequence ends with ORTON *and* HALLIWELL *on a balcony at sunset. They kiss.*

INT. APARTMENT, TANGIER. DAY. 1967
Sound of typing. HALLIWELL *enters the apartment.*
HALLIWELL: Why do you have to work? Enjoy yourself.
ORTON: I am enjoying myself. Listen to this.
HALLIWELL: I don't want to. Not here. There's going to be
     enough of this when we get back to London.
     (ORTON *goes on typing.*)
     Stop it!
ORTON: Piss off.
     (HALLIWELL *seizes the typewriter and throws it off the
     balcony.*)
     You stupid nutter.
     (*A* BOY *watches, horrified.*)
HALLIWELL: When we get back to London we're finished. This
     is the end.
ORTON: Why don't you add, 'I'm going back to mother.'
HALLIWELL: That's the kind of line that makes your plays
     ultimately worthless.
     (*The* BOY *is speechless.*)
ORTON: (*Wearily*) He's waiting to be paid.
     (*The* BOY *looks at* ORTON.)
     Actually he's rather sweet. I think I shall retire to lick my
     wounds. (*Taking the* BOY's *hand*) Or have them licked
     for me.
     (HALLIWELL *weeps.*)

INT. ORTON AND HALLIWELL'S FLAT. NIGHT. 1967

The door is pushed back. ORTON *comes in, picks up the pile of mail behind the door. He turns on the light, puts his case down and starts opening his letters.* HALLIWELL *comes in with cases and a bottle of milk.*

HALLIWELL: You might open the curtains. This place stinks.

(*He opens the window, then takes the milk into the kitchen.*)

ORTON: That's good. Peggy's sold the Beatles script to someone else. I get paid twice over apparently.

(HALLIWELL *bangs something down in the kitchen.*

ORTON *registers this, but goes on.*)

The *Observer* would like to interview me.

(*Another bang.*)

And *Vogue* wonders if I'd be interested in modelling some clothes. So much for the holiday.

HALLIWELL: What?

ORTON: I take you away for four weeks. We come back and you're still the same miserable, jealous bitch you were before we went. Have you got them out? You have, haven't you. I know you.

(ORTON *gets up and* HALLIWELL *tries to hide the bottle of pills he has taken from the cupboard.*)

HALLIWELL: Joe.

ORTON: Come on. Do your act. Count them out.

(*He sets out the pills.* HALLIWELL *tries to get at them, but* ORTON *holds him off.*)

How many is it, the fatal dose? Twelve, is it? One, two, three.

HALLIWELL: I'll do it one of these days, you'll see.

ORTON: You never have so far, ducky.

(*He hurls a tablet across the room.*)

Fetch. Fetch.

(HALLIWELL *chases it.*)

And another.

(*The telephone rings.*)

Answer that.

HALLIWELL: No.

ORTON: Answer it.

HALLIWELL: Yes. Hello, Leonie. Yes, very nice thank you. Hold on.

ORTON: Hello. When was this? Does that mean there'll have to be a funeral? Shit.
(*He looks at his watch. He puts the phone down.*)
My mother's dead.

HALLIWELL: Oh. Joe. I know what it's like. My whole life changed when my mother died. I'm sorry.

ORTON: I'm not.
(*He starts getting ready.*)
And while I'm away you should see a doctor. A proper doctor. You're sick.

INT. FAYHURST ROAD. DAY. 1967
The Orton home. The family sits in the living room. ORTON, *Orton's two sisters* LEONIE *and* MARILYN, *his brother* DOUGLAS *and* WILLIAM ORTON, *his father.* LEONIE *is pregnant.* GEORGE BARNETT, *her husband, is there.* ORTON *sits next to* LEONIE *and nudges her and she giggles. The* UNDERTAKER *appears.*

UNDERTAKER: Mother's ready now if you'd like to come in and pay your respects.
(*They all get up.*)
Father first.
(WILLIAM ORTON *has been sitting unnoticed by the fire. They get him up. He goes in first and they file into the sitting room after him.* MARILYN *nudges her husband and mouths 'cigarette'. He puts it out.* ELSIE *lies in an open coffin, an* UNDERTAKER'S BOY *standing by the wall with the coffin lid.* ORTON *files in after* LEONIE.)

LEONIE: (*Just before they get in*) Stop it, Joe. I don't want to laugh. I didn't love her, but I don't want to laugh.

MARILYN: I still don't know why you want to go calling yourself Joe. John's a much classier name.

ORTON: You've left her glasses off.

UNDERTAKER: You'll find that's normal procedure. Generally speaking, people prefer it.

ORTON: What's happened to her teeth?

UNDERTAKER: Mislaid apparently.

ORTON: Shame. She was proud of her teeth.
> (*They file out. The* UNDERTAKER'S BOY, *whom* ORTON *eyes, waiting to put the coffin lid on.*)

UNDERTAKER: This is mother's nightgown.

MARILYN: I don't want it. A thing like that.

LEONIE: Someone ought to have it.

DOUGLAS: Chuck it out.

LEONIE: That's no way to talk. Not dead five minutes and it's into the bin with her nightie.

UNDERTAKER: If you leave it with me I'll dispose of it. We pass them on to old folks. Many of them are quite grateful.

LEONIE: Joe. Take Dad to spend a penny. We don't want him having an accident in the car. Go with John, Dad.

DOUGLAS: How long will this affair go on?

MARILYN: Why?

DOUGLAS: I'm running a business.

INT. FAYHURST ROAD: LAVATORY. DAY. 1967
ORTON takes his FATHER's *trousers down, leaving them round his ankles.*

ORTON: Come on, Dad. Hold it, Dad.
> (WILLIAM *doesn't.* ORTON *has to hold his* FATHER's *cock and aim for him.*)

WILLIAM: What are you doing?
> (WILLIAM *turns and looks into his* SON's *face.*)

INT. FAYHURST ROAD. DAY. 1967
The coffin is just being carried out of the room and into the hearse. They all stand up.

UNDERTAKER: I think just father's tribute on the coffin.

ORTON: Simple, but effective.

LEONIE: (*Quietly*) I'll kill you, Joe, if you don't stop it.

MARILYN: Dash yourself off, Duggie. You're covered in scurf.

EXT. FAYHURST ROAD. DAY. 1967
The RELATIVES *go down the garden path to the waiting cars.* PEOPLE *watching.*

66

INT. FAYHURST ROAD: BEDROOM. DAY. 1967
LEONIE *enters.* ORTON *has been going through the dressing-table drawers. He holds his hand out to* LEONIE. *In it are his mother's false teeth.*
LEONIE: Chuck them away.
ORTON: I want something to remember her by.
> (*He puts them in his pocket.*)
LEONIE: You've no feeling at all, you.
> (*She is clearing out another drawer.*)
> I've started night school now. Modern English Literature. (*Pause.*) It's amazing how many writers are queer.
> (ORTON *doesn't react. She goes on clearing out the drawer, whilst* ORTON *sits in front of his mother's dressing table and alters the mirrors so that he can see himself three ways.*)
> Do you think Mum was why you liked lads?
ORTON: Lay off.
> (*He goes downstairs. She follows him.*)

INT. FAYHURST ROAD: SITTING ROOM. DAY. 1967
LEONIE: You do look at lads. I've seen you.
ORTON: I've had a better time then they had (*in heavy inverted commas*) 'sexually'.
WILLIAM: We had no time at all.
> (*Pause.*)
LEONIE: There must have been times when you were happy.
WILLIAM: Oh yes. Several.
> (*Pause before the cut to next morning.*)

EXT. FAYHURST ROAD. DAY. 1967
LEONIE *and* ORTON *go out to the garden gate.*
ORTON: I don't expect it'll be long before I'm back.
LEONIE: Why?
ORTON: He's not going to last long, is he?
> (*He kisses her. She smiles.*)
LEONIE: You kiss now. You never used to kiss. That's London.
> (*He walks down the street, turns and calls back.*)
ORTON: I never told you. I met Paul McCartney.

EXT. LEICESTER BUS STOP. DAY. 1967
ORTON *waits at a bus stop. A* LABOURER *comes by. Not a dish. He looks at* ORTON. ORTON *notes the look.*

INT/EXT. DERELICT HOUSE: LEICESTER. DAY. 1967
ORTON *and the* LABOURER *are crossing a piece of waste ground towards some derelict houses. They go into one of them. No door. No windows. Surrounded by a bleak landscape of cleared sites and distant factories.*
LABOURER: Thought you were a bobby at first. Black tie.
ORTON: Funeral.
LABOURER: Who died?
    (ORTON *has undone his trousers and let them fall.*)
ORTON: Mother and two sisters. Dead in the fire that consumed our home.
LABOURER: You must be heartbroken.
ORTON: I am. Handle my balls.
    (*The* LABOURER *does so, then goes out of shot.* ORTON *lifts his arms above his head and stretches. He yawns. It should be very bleak.*)

INT. CRITERION THEATRE: WINGS. NIGHT. 1967
We hear the actors doing Loot *on the stage and* SIMON WARD *is waiting to make his entrance when* ORTON *appears.*
SIMON WARD: Sorry.
ORTON: What about?
SIMON WARD: Your mother.
ORTON: Have you got to the prop teeth?
    (SIMON WARD *takes them out.* ORTON *takes them.*)
SIMON WARD: Don't mess about. I'm on.
    (ORTON *takes out his mother's teeth and gives them to* SIMON WARD. *He looks at them.*)
ORTON: My mum's teeth.
SIMON WARD: Jesus Christ.
STAGE MANAGER: You're on.
    (*She pushes* SIMON WARD *on to the stage.* SIMON WARD *is so confused, looking at the teeth in his hand, that he forgets his words and the* STAGE MANAGER *has to prompt. He looks*

furiously at ORTON, *who is watching through a hole in the scenery and laughing.*)

INT. ORTON AND HALLIWELL'S FLAT. NIGHT. 1967
HALLIWELL *is on the telephone.*
PEGGY: (*Voice over*) It wasn't a rational act.
LAHR: (*Voice over*) Well, obviously.
PEGGY: (*Voice over*) I didn't mean that. These things happen, that's all.
(ORTON *is getting into bed.*)
HALLIWELL: (*On the phone*) I've an appointment with the psychiatrist at ten tomorrow. Yes. Thank you for all the trouble you've taken.
(HALLIWELL *puts the phone down.*)
ORTON: You don't want a psychiatrist. It's this room. We've lived here too long.
HALLIWELL: So? I keep finding places. You won't even go look. (*Seizes a newspaper.*) 'Two bedrooms, two reception rooms, patio and bathroom. This well-proportioned accommodation can be maintained with the minimum effort, thereby leaving more time for leisure pursuits.'
ORTON: Where?
HALLIWELL: East Croydon.
ORTON: I won't live in East Croydon.
HALLIWELL: You're so unadventurous. I like the country. It would be nice to see the occasional green field.
ORTON: In East Croydon?
HALLIWELL: Anywhere. Not you. You'd be content to trail up and down the Pentonville Road till your balls dropped off.
ORTON: What did the doctor say?
HALLIWELL: He's already talking about hospital and I haven't even seen the psychiatrist yet. Still he's a very good doctor. He treats cabinet ministers.
ORTON: What happens if we split up?
HALLIWELL: How would that help me? We're talking about *me*.
ORTON: Well, we can't go on like this.
HALLIWELL: I've given you everything. I made you.
ORTON: I'm not Eliza fucking Doolittle. I made myself.

HALLIWELL: These are my books.

ORTON: I'd see you all right.

HALLIWELL: I taught you.

ORTON: I taught you too.

HALLIWELL: What? How to go into a public lavatory?

ORTON: Anyway, if I hadn't met you it would have been someone else. Sleep on it.

HALLIWELL: How?

ORTON: I could give you a wank.

(HALLIWELL *groans*.)

Well, what do you want?

HALLIWELL: Joe. John.

ORTON: I'm not John. John's dead.

(*Turns to go to sleep*.)

If you change your mind about the wank don't wake me up.

(*Pause*.)

HALLIWELL: Joe.

(*No answer.* HALLIWELL *sits at* ORTON's *desk*.) I don't understand my life. I was an only child. I lost both my parents. By the time I was twenty I was bald. I'm homosexual. In the way of circumstances and background to transcend I had everything an artist could possibly want. It was practically a blueprint. I was programmed to be a novelist or a playwright. But I'm not. And you are.

(HALLIWELL *gets his suicide pills and arranges them on the desk. He goes to the tool box and gets a hammer. He stands looking at* ORTON *asleep*.)

You do everything better than me. You even sleep better than me.

(*Possibly* ORTON *wakes up as* HALLIWELL *hits him, starting up shouting, 'You stupid nutter!' The hammer comes down several times,* ORTON's *blood splattering over the collage*.)

INT. ORTON AND HALLIWELL'S FLAT. 1967

HALLIWELL *sees the* Evening Standard *award on the desk*.

HALLIWELL: I should have used that. More theatrical. You'd have spotted that straight away.

(*He writes a note and then adds a PS and props it neatly on the*

diary. It reads : If you read his diary all will be explained. K.H.
P.S. Especially the latter part. *Halliwell picks up the pills and
the grapefruit juice and looks at the camera.*) I loved him. I must
have loved him. I chose him to kill me.
(*He swallows the pills and drinks the juice.*) Joe. John.
(*He lies down leaving the frame empty. The camera pulls back
from the room.* ORTON'S *body,* HALLIWELL *dead. Sunlight
streaming in through the window.*)

INT. ORTON AND HALLIWELL'S FLAT. DAY. 1967
*The door of the flat from the inside. The telephone rings inside the flat.
Close in on the keyhole of the door. An eye looking.*

INT. ORTON AND HALLIWELL'S FLAT. LANDING.
DAY. 1967
Outside door. A uniformed CHAUFFEUR *is peering in through the
keyhole watched by* MRS SUGDEN.
MRS SUGDEN: They're not away. It's not five minutes since
    they got back from Tangier.
CHAUFFEUR: I was scheduled to pick him up at twelve.
    A private lunch.
MRS SUGDEN: He leads an increasingly glamorous life.
CHAUFFEUR: Is he a heavy sleeper?
MRS SUGDEN: I know nothing about his personal life. Idle
    curiosity has never been my strong point. Try looking
    through the letterbox.
CHAUFFEUR: There's a coat.
    (*Cut to the inside of the door.*)
MRS SUGDEN: (*Voice over*) One moment while I fetch an
    implement.
    (*The coat is pushed aside by the long bicycle pump. The*
    CHAUFFEUR'S *eyes at the letter box.*)
    Do you know Mr Orton?
CHAUFFEUR: Not personally. I have driven him in the firm's car
    to different destinations.
    Has the other got a bald head?
MRS SUGDEN: No. He wears a wig.
CHAUFFEUR: Can we break down this door?

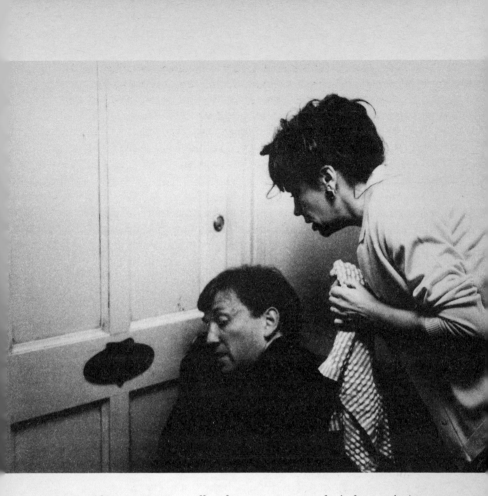

(MRS SUGDEN *calls to her* HUSBAND, *who is downstairs.*)
MRS SUGDEN: Clifford, can we break down this door?
MR SUGDEN: Certainly not. If there is damage to be done call
the police. That's their job.

INT. ORTON AND HALLIWELL'S FLAT. DAY. 1967
The door is immediately broken down. A POLICE INSPECTOR *in a
raincoat and trilby, like Truscott in* Loot, *comes in.*

EXT. NOEL ROAD. DAY. 1967
We see PEGGY *arrive by car. She goes upstairs. As the* INSPECTOR

73

and PHOTOGRAPHER *arrive,* PEGGY *comes downstairs and leaves.*

INT. MORTUARY. DAY. 1967
PEGGY, LEONIE *and* DOUGLAS ORTON. PEGGY *has one urn.*
An ATTENDANT *comes in with another.*

PEGGY: (*Voice over*) There were two ceremonies. Joe's at Golders
    Green, everybody there. House full. Ken's at Enfield, you
    couldn't give tickets away.

LAHR: (*Voice over*) That's sad.

PEGGY: (*Voice over*) Well, they finished up together at the end.

ATTENDANT: Strictly speaking, we would have preferred it if
    both the deceased had been cremated on the premises.
    Intermingling would then have been carried out by
    experienced personnel under controlled conditions.
    (*He pushes the urn across to* PEGGY, *plus another empty urn.*
    Also a scoop. LEONIE *begins to scoop ashes from each urn into*
    the third.)

LEONIE: I think I'm putting in more of Joe than I am of
    Kenneth.

PEGGY: It's a gesture, dear, not a recipe.

DOUGLAS: I hope nobody hears about this in Leicester.

EXT. MORTUARY GARDEN. DAY. 1967
A long shot of them scattering the ashes.

INT. PEGGY RAMSAY'S OFFICE. DAY. THE PRESENT

LAHR: If he hadn't murdered Joe nobody would ever have
    known his name.

PEGGY: Ken was the first wife. They do all the work, the waiting,
    and then . . .

LAHR: First wives don't beat their husbands' heads in.

PEGGY: No. Though why not I can't think.

LAHR: So what does that make you? The second wife?

PEGGY: Better than that, dear. The widow.
    (*She switches off the tape recorder.*)
    Have you ever seen the flat?
    (LAHR *shakes his head.*)

INT. ORTON AND HALLIWELL'S FLAT. DAY.
THE PRESENT. PEGGY, LAHR, ANTHEA *and* YOUNG
COUPLE.

PEGGY: These days I could make a living just talking about Joe.
Theatre conferences, gay groups. Arts programmes. When
those who have known the famous are publicly debriefed of
their memories, knowing as their own dusk falls that they
will only be remembered for remembering someone else.

YOUNG MAN: Is that all? Have you seen all you want?
(*He opens the door for them and they leave. The* YOUNG MAN
glances glumly at his WIFE *before coming back into the room. He
closes the door and goes out of shot. We hold on the closed door as
the film ends.*)